ESSAYS ON THE
DOT-COM
RETAIL
PHENOMENON:
1996-2001

TENSER'S TIRADES

by

James Tenser
Founder of VStoreNews.com

ISBN: 978-0-7596-3804-4 (sc)
ISBN: 978-0-7596-3803-7 (e)

Print information available on the last page.

1stBooks – rev. 09/09/22

Tenser's Tirades documents the obsession of self-styled author/consultant/evangelist James Tenser with the astonishing phenomenon of dot-com retailing. This collection of 32 essays appeared over a period of about five years in a dozen leading retail trade periodicals. Collectively, they track the early promise, exhilarating rise and stunning demise of born-for-the-Web retailing through a series of snapshots taken in the moment. As one of the earliest observers to grasp and comment upon the unvarnished realities of e-retailing, Tenser was right more often than he was wrong, but as these rants reveal, he never kept his opinions to himself.

Published in the United States by 1St Books Library.

Grateful acknowledgement is made to the following for permission to reprint previously published material:

Accessories and *MR* magazines (Business Journals, Inc., New York, NY) for "Your Dot-Com Response: Compete, Collaborate or Consume?

Brand Marketing (Fairchild Publications, New York) for "CRM For Fun and Profit", "E-Business As Usual", "Next Y2K Challenge: Packaging e-Solutions", "Virtually Ready"

Chain Store Age (Lebhar-Friedman, New York) for "Beyond Multichannel Retail"

eRetailing World (Bill Communications, New York) for "Will Deals Bolster Online Grocery?"

Executive Technology (Fairchild Publications, New York) for "When Bits Meet Mortar", "The End of the Beginning"

Ideations (Design Forum, New York) for "Touchpoint Integration — Challenge for Web-Enabled Retailers"

Nexgenix, Inc. (Irvine, CA) for "When To Say No"

RetailTech magazine (Bill Communications, New York) for "All Retailing is Eretailing"

RT magazine (Bill Communications, New York) for "Established Drug Merchants: Virtually Unstoppable", "Virtual Retailing Must Deliver Real Value"

Sales & Marketing Quarterly (Association of Sales & Marketing Companies, Reston, VA) for "Why Virtual Stores Mean Real Dollars"

VStoreNews ® (James Tenser, Norwalk, CT) for "Broadband Merchants: When All Retailing is e-Retailing", "Pulp! (Not Fiction)", "The Art of Politax", "Take Your Web Portal and Stick It!", "In Webhouse Club, Priceline Invokes a Namesake", "Embrace Complexity, Stupid!", "Yes, Dulles, Virginia. There IS a Sanity Clause", "HTTP, Holiday Hype and Heraldry", "Beyond Portals and Communities — Vstores", "Shampoo's Swell, But Can You Email an Egg Cream?", "Margin To Hell (For a Heavenly Cause)", "Are You Ready for The Next Channel?"

http://www.vstorenews.com

Manufactured in the United States of America

This 1st Books Library edition is printed on acid free paper

FOR MINDY

(WHO SURELY KNOWS A
TIRADE WHEN SHE HEARS ONE)

THANK YOU FOR ALL
YOU HAVE BEEN TO ME

On Persistence:

"To open a shop is easy. To keep it open is an art."

— *Confucius*

"Reality is merely an illusion, albeit a very persistent one."

— *Albert Einstein*

FOREWORD

VIRTUAL STORE REALITY

IT'S EASY ENOUGH NOW to recognize the inherent flaws in the dot-com retail propositions which flooded the American marketplace between 1996 and 2000. Here were product marketing businesses invented by young e-turks who were infatuated by the promise of emerging Internet technology, but almost charmingly naive about the real subtleties of branding, merchandising, fulfillment, supply-chain logistics and consumer psychology.

These "dot-com whiz kids," as I have disparagingly labeled this class of Web entrepreneurs, were led down the fantasy path by a cadre of venture capitalists whose degree of avarice was well matched to their level of self-delusion.

Breathlessly following them were a whole herd of analysts and stock market investors who bought in to the delirious fantasy of the New Economy while requiring little more justification for their bets than some favorable "buzz" and their ability to point their browsers at the home page of the next hot IPO.

Not that I have any opinion about this... :)

The truth is we were all of us fooled, to a greater or lesser extent, by the pleasant belief that Web technology would engender a new virtual store reality, in which many of the old rules for doing business would be discarded in favor of a new order. Like lumbering dinosaurs, Big Dumb Companies would whither, while the quick, clever, mammals of Silicon Valley would devour their eggs and multiply until they dominated the planet.

In 1996 I was a believer too. I boldly declared that online retailing — virtual stores — were "the next new channel" of retail trade. I forecast a revolution in the way products came to market. I predicted that gross margins would come under new and greater pressure as a result of the inherently efficient selling processes made possible by the Internet.

I believed this so strongly and completely that I plotted to leave a perfectly good and prestigious job as managing editor of a well-respected trade magazine, *Brand Marketing*, and set out to build a new information business which focused exclusively on what I in a moment of unchecked hubris chose to coin as the "Vstore."

In the spring of 1998 I launched *VStoreNews*, and its companion Web site, vstorenews.com, at that time the first knowledge business exclusively devoted to covering the new online retail trade. Consistent with my views of the new virtual world, this publication was distributed only electronically — that is by email (or fax for those few Luddites willing to invest in a subscription).

As I assumed the role of self-styled evangelist and full-time observer of the new retailing marketplace, I also sought to practice a new type of advocacy journalism — one that favored candid opinion over guarded objectivity. Whether they agree or disagree, I decided my audience would view the facts through the lens of a forthright point of view. My target readers, after all, are intelligent beings, quite capable of deciding for themselves whether the views expressed in *VStoreNews* were worthy. Besides, I was sure I was right.

Each edition of *VStoreNews* began with a kind of editorial rant, for which I chose an alliterative header. "Tenser's Tirades" were intended to be the highlight of the e-letter, the branding vehicle, the thing that made *VStoreNews* stand apart from the wave of Internet retailing periodicals which flooded the scene before the end of that year.

Within three months of the *VStoreNews* launch, the media discovered e-retailing with a vengeance. By the summer of 1998, every major magazine and newspaper had begun covering the dot-com phenomenon and I found my area of specialization to be in demand. My editorial colleagues in the retail trade press began calling, and soon I was contributing guest columns to a variety of magazines.

Alarmed by the dot-com media hysteria of the 1998-1999 period and against the backdrop of a skyrocketing NASDAQ, I tried to use these soapboxes which were so generously offered to present a more reasoned interpretation of the fast moving events in the virtual retailing sector. I found myself cast in the role of futurist/contrarian, and began to realize that my initial interpretation of the online retailing phenomenon was in need of fresh analysis.

I began to offer an alternate view of the New Retailing which portrayed Internet-enabled selling not as a new competing class of retail trade, but as a new and revolutionary skill set which would soon permeate traditional retail businesses and change their underlying economics forever.

The outcome of the battle between the "dot-cons" and the "brick-and-mortals" would be determined in the end by the bursting of the NASDAQ bubble in April 2000. Suddenly, the inflated values of the born-for-the-Web players were deflated, and shrewd traditional retailers began to acquire their assets and techniques and fold them into their much stronger, more sustainable businesses.

The success of a few strong players such as Amazon.com and eBay notwithstanding, the decline of the pure-play Internet retailers has been nearly as breathtaking as their initial heady climb. To the credit of the confident dot-com kids who had declared, "This changes everything," nearly everything has changed — only not in the ways they predicted.

Today, retailing is clearly a multichannel activity, one that melds online and off-line channels into a unified customer experience. Virtual stores and physical stores may look the same as they ever did, but the information technologies which power their operations behind the scenes continue to undergo dramatic changes.

This book is a compilation of my published commentary about the virtual retailing phenomenon during the period from 1996 until the present. I have arranged the 33 articles in reverse chronological order, so that reading this book should be a bit like a trip back in Internet time.

It is my sincere hope that this compendium begins to reveal a key insight about the sheer might of the World Wide Web, which has almost magically compressed the lifetime of a profound business phenomenon into a mere half decade.

CONTENTS

This essay is intended as a call to action for chain retailers. It was published in Executive Technology *magazine, March 2001.*

THE END OF THE BEGINNING

AS IF WE'RE SUPPOSED TO BE SURPRISED, the same business writers who one year ago proclaimed the end of retailing as we know it are now nodding their collective heads in mock sadness over widespread implosion of the dot-coms.

It is certainly entertaining to witness dramatic plunges in stock prices and the comeuppance of arrogant venture capitalists and dot-com kids. Once again, however, the analysts and writers are focused mainly on the gory details and missing the larger picture.

The online retailing boom is hardly over. It is hardly even slowing down. U.S. retail e-commerce tripled in 2000 versus 1999 to $45 billion, according to estimates published recently by Jupiter Research. Wired Americans now number 122 million, approaching half the U.S. population.

There are even leading indicators of profits on the horizon: The ratio of marketing spending to revenue declined by a third from 79% in third quarter 1999 to 47% in third quarter 2000, according to *The Industry Standard.* Other indicators confirm that so-called customer acquisition costs are declining. Online hours per family are increasing. Email message counts continue to leap upwards.

These bullish metrics appear to belie the recent negativity of the NASDAQ nabobs. If online retailing continues to have a strong outlook, where has all the value gone?

A look at online retailing's leader board begins to reveal the answer: While a handful of born-for-the-Web retailers — eBay, Amazon, — remain in strong shape, most of the top 50 now are traditional retailers with online branches.

> Shrewd retailers will ferret out this value and obtain it at the current attractive prices so as to instantly add sophisticated online merchandising capability to their existing businesses.

The best of the best online — Eddie Bauer, Office Depot, Micro Warehouse, JC Penney, L.L. Bean, Barnes & Noble and a host of others — all share this multichannel heritage. Many were successful catalogers first. Others began with robust specialty chains.

Executives from JC Penney and Eddie Bauer are on record confirming that their three-channel shoppers (Web, catalog, store) are far and away their largest and most profitable customers. This is a most opportune moment for other strong chains to emulate them.

Some 18 months ago I forecast that traditional retailers would soon see an opportunity to acquire the technology, know-how, inventory, brands and customer lists of down-on-their-heels dot-com retailers for cents on the dollar.

Well, that opportunity has come to pass. With the dot-com dream collapsing, online retailers' market valuations have plunged, and their viability is imperiled. Traditional retailers are well positioned to pick up the pieces.

When online grocery pioneer Streamline.com announced its shutdown in early November, it disappointed a core group of happy customers who loved the service. Ahold USA kicked the tires, but declined to buy. So Streamline, its know-how and its loyal customer relationships, simply ceased to exist on Nov. 22.

Pets.com cashed it in a few weeks earlier. Despite strong brand recognition, and a quality functioning site, it had not found a suitor. Last we heard it was trying to auction off its sock puppet mascot.

But as CVS drugstores proved when it acquired Soma.com in the spring of 1999, and as Ahold and Safeway each underscored when they made their respective investments in Peapod.com and GroceryWorks.com, there is significant value in some failing dot-coms.

Shrewd retailers will ferret out this value and obtain it at the current attractive prices so as to instantly add sophisticated online merchandising capability to their existing businesses. Integrating the technology (and cultures) is a non-trivial challenge, but there is good help available from e-business consulting firms (who are pretty negotiable at the moment too).

Retail decision-makers would do well to shop boldly while the fire sale is on. This is truly the end of the beginning. Now comes the golden age of online retailing.

This feature article was written to provide an overview of Customer Relationship Management for manufacturers and marketers of consumer goods. It was originally published in Brand Marketing *magazine, January 2001.*

CRM FOR FUN AND PROFIT

Web-enabled customer relationship management is all the rage in the New Economy, and brand marketers are beginning to embrace these principles.

MID-TWENTIETH CENTURY petroleum baron J. Paul Getty once quipped that he possessed three secrets to success in business: The first, he said, was to work harder than everybody else. His second bit of advice was even more profound: "Work smarter than everybody else." But it was the third piece of wisdom that made Getty a billionaire:

"Find oil."

Mineral wealth is a fine thing. But for brand marketers in the 21st century, value is based largely on other, less tangible assets. Brand equity comes prominently to mind. So does an established network of retailers and distributors.

With the rise and acceptance of Web-based commerce and marketing, consumer relationships are gaining prominence as a new form of "oil" for brand marketers. Call it a corollary of the dot-com principle: Increasingly sophisticated technology enables a new emphasis on customer care, one-to-few and one-to-one contact, quality, service and customization under the collective banner of customer relationship management — CRM.

"All this adds up to a new measurement of value — *customer equity* {italics theirs} — that reflects the value of customer relationships and the contribution they make to a company's future growth prospects," Phil Tamminga and Pat O'Halloran of Andersen Consulting's Global CRM Practice wrote recently in the *Cutter IT Journal.*

They continued, "Companies that have not invested in developing specific CRM capabilities are leaving millions of dollars of profit on the table."

The promise of Web-enabled customer relationship management (eCRM) is invoked by consultants, technologists, software firms and academics who envision a new future, empowered by Internet technology to enable "one-to-one" marketing, enhance service and sustain long-term value.

"Companies can boost profits by almost 75% by retaining just 5% or more of their customers," loyalty expert Frederick Reichheld, director at Bain & Company, wrote in the *Harvard Business Review.*

"The smartest of the smart will shift their growth strategies away from new customer acquisition and toward building and broadening their relationships with the good customers they've already won," he added.

With words like these surely ringing in their ears, several of the nation's most powerful multi-brand manufacturers are now drilling into the latent value in consumer database records previously obtained through promotion redemptions, call-center records, warranty registrations, requests for product usage advice and Web site registrations.

As a matter of brand marketing fact and legend, over the past decade Procter & Gamble, Nestle, Philip Morris, Johnson & Johnson and other consumer goods leaders have each accumulated tens of millions of data records identifying consumers who have had some interaction with their brands. Those lists are prized and protected and have been occasionally tapped for promotions. But compiling a large database is not the same thing as maintaining a portfolio of profitable consumer relationships.

These companies are currently wrestling with a set of issues that affects nearly every consumer products company in America today: How to economically establish and maintain consumer relationships and consumer knowledge? How to leverage e-business technique to advance your interests without alienating traditional trade channels? Indeed, how to turn these actions into a source of added value for your retail customers?

Where we saw innovative but relatively primitive use of brand consumer databases during the 1990s for such purposes as co-marketing and direct mail, there are now concerted efforts to go further, to identify the most valuable customers across multiple brands and establish profitable, ongoing relationships with them.

Because of the low communication costs associated with targeted email, Web-based CRM technology looks attractive to many brand marketers. Software products such as e-Piphany, Kana, and Yesmail provide strong front-end tools for Web-based direct marketing, while data warehouse solutions built on such platforms as Oracle or Microsoft SQL Server provide capability for handling the immense quantities of data which must be captured, sifted and interpreted for eCRM to work.

> Mineral wealth is a fine thing. But for brand marketers in the 21st century, value is based largely on other, less tangible assets.

Major e-business application suite providers, such as Broadvision and Vignette, are adding these competencies into their newest version offerings, in the hope of capturing the high-end of the burgeoning market for integrated CRM solutions.

Research organization IDC estimates that in 1999 corporate spending on CRM software licenses and maintenance grew 71% to $3.3 billion in 1999. IDC forecasts that this figure will grow to $12.1 billion in 2004, for a CAGR (cumulative annual growth rate) of 30%. North America accounted for 70% of 1999 CRM licenses.

AMR Research projects even faster growth, with licenses increasing from \$4.4 billion in 1999 to \$24.6 billion in 2004 for a CAGR of 45%.

When Peppers & Rogers Group fielded its "CRM Census" this Fall, 42% of respondents across a variety of industries indicated that their companies currently have formal CRM programs in place. Of the 58% who did not, nearly nine in ten indicated that they would implement CRM by 2002.

Asked to indicate their agreement with several alternate definitions of CRM, 65% said it reflected a "move from being product-centric to customer-centric." Half the respondents indicated that CRM is about "using IT tools that achieve incremental business improvements." Four in ten said CRM involves "making integrated customer contact information available in near real time to all customer contact personnel."

In Peppers & Rogers survey, 42% of respondents across a variety of industries indicated that their companies currently have formal CRM programs in place.

As a general rule, brand marketers' database marketing efforts to date fall far short of these ideals. Rarely has there been any data synchronization between brand groups across the company. Often, individual brands within the same organization employ different database technologies. In many cases, even the data record structures are incompatible.

This is in part an artifact of the brand system, which has tended to encourage a "silo" mentality among brand managers. But it may be attributed in at least equal part to technology challenges and a narrow understanding of the purpose and potential of interactive and database marketing.

"Many marketing people still pursue interactive sales solely for their immediate cash return rather than the contribution they can also make to brand values," Sir Martin Sorrell, Chief Executive of WPP Group plc, one of the world's largest communications companies, wrote recently. "Hence 'loyalty' programmes [sic] which have nothing to do with real loyalty."

Sorrell seems here to imply that the aforementioned customer equity can be a component of brand equity. How do capital markets assign value to brand marketers? Certainly this is a question of ongoing strategic importance.

Companies with high market valuations have greater access to the capital that funds innovation and growth. They enjoy greater shareholder confidence and support. They tend to reward their leaders better.

Tangible assets — cash, inventory, facilities, mineral wealth — have been recognized as sources of value for centuries. But the focus of value is shifting away from tangible "stuff" and toward intangible "idea-based" assets.

Intellectual properties — patents, licenses, trademarks, and trade secrets — are arguably the assets of the 20th century. Below this heading lies brand equity, a specialized form of intellectual property that has grown to great prominence in the past half-century.

"Internet-enabled customer relationships are joining brands and intellectual property among the new assets that define the value of brand marketing businesses today."

Internet-enabled customer relationships are joining brands and intellectual property among the new assets that define the value of brand marketing businesses today.

Web-centered data collection, data warehousing, data synchronization, data mining and direct marketing are must-have techniques for fostering profitable customer relationships. These activities pose new challenges for consumer-centric marketers as they chart a path to prevail in the emerging business environment.

This is not what some have called disintermediation or "Consumer Direct." That is, eCRM for brand marketers is not necessarily about selling merchandise direct to the consumer by end-running the retailer. Indeed, for most manufacturers such a tactic would destroy critical traditional supply chain relationships. Home Depot's 1999 ultimatum no doubt still rings in the ears of Rubbermaid, Stanley, Black & Decker their kin (quoting loosely): "If you sell to consumers on your web site, your products are off our shelves."

No, eCRM is about maintaining consumer relationships that should enhance Home Depot's ability to sell more of your drills, hammers or wastebaskets. It's about pre-selling your brand to your best consumers so the retailer doesn't have to. Nothing revolutionary about that.

At the end of the day, the most valuable company is the one with the most profitable portfolio of consumer relationships.

For Multi-Brand Marketers, CRM Begins With Synchronization

The value of Customer Relationship Management is twofold, according to an October 24, 2000 report by Merrill Lynch:

- CRM enables companies to be more responsive to their customers; and
- It lets organizations integrate disparate channels and functions so they can understand their customers' needs and develop more profitable, longer-term customer relationships.

For brand marketers, integration of customer data may be extended not only within each brand, but also across multiple brands. This is no mean feat, but it may bring rich dividends.

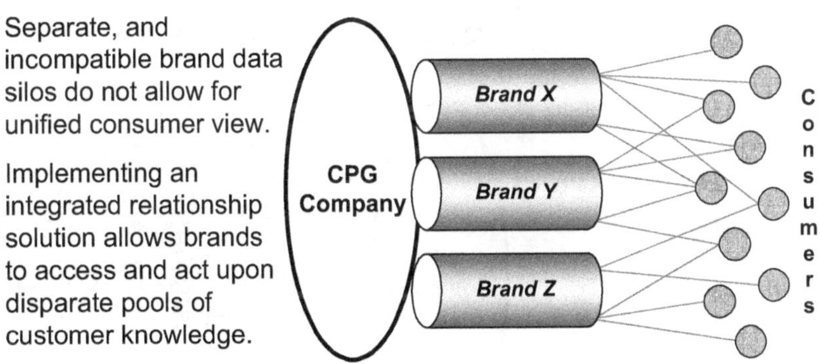

Under their present database marketing setups, multi-brand marketers rarely can discern which consumers who buy one their brands also buy another. Clearly the consumer who buys several of your brands represents a high-value relationship, one which may deserve differential treatment versus the consumer who buys only one of your products.

Moreover, within the group of consumers who buy one brand there is likely a subset whose characteristics match with the loyal consumers of another brand. How may relationship equity be leveraged across multiple brands so that customized, targeted offerings may be communicated to motivate multi-brand purchasing?

Integration within a data warehouse is a key requisite for this to occur. For companies with existing simple databases compiled from warranty, promotion redemption and other sources, there is a modest technical challenge here. Data must be extracted from the existing (and often incompatible) databases, transformed into a common format, and then loaded into the overarching warehouse before data synchronization may occur.

This extract-transform-load (ETL) process may be structured to align with the way a brand marketer already views consumer data. Spectra Marketing's widely employed lifestyle-lifestage grid comes to mind here.

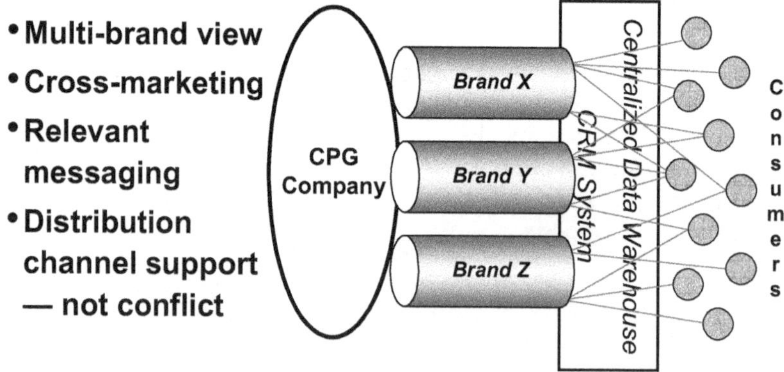

Collating multi-brand consumer data in this fashion may reveal a subset of consumers who are already loyal to more than one brand in a company's portfolio. These are clearly of higher total value than single brand loyalists, justifying higher levels of communications, incentive and reward.

"Different customers really are different. But to be fair, and visibly fair, a company needs to have business standards and definitions of customer differentiation — standards that net customers top one-to-one service no matter who they are," personalization guru Don Peppers wrote recently in his company's newsletter *Inside 1 to 1*.

"Treating everyone the same is not only inefficient, but also the poorest form of customer service."

TENSER'S TIRADES

Some more advice for brand marketers as they weigh the multiple concurrent requirements for new e-business technology. This article was originally published in Brand Marketing *magazine without the sidebars and charts, which we have restored here. The four-dimensional taxonomy referenced herein was developed by Nexgenix, Inc. during my tenure there.*

E-Business As Usual

On-line marketing software is rapidly becoming a necessity rather than a luxury. But discrete objectives must be combined into a comprehensive strategy to ensure success.

Let's dial back about a half-century in Internet time — to the summer of 1999: We began to hear firsthand reports from brand marketers as diverse as Best Foods, Del Monte Fresh Produce, Nabisco and Procter & Gamble about some intriguing requests. All confirmed that some of their largest chain retail customers had asked them to provide e-business solutions within their respective categories.

These "requests" were delivered on terms that seemed familiar to veterans of the "category management" movement — with a carrot in one hand and a stick in the other. The intimation was that the supplier who could bring a turnkey solution for online business to bear in time for the Nov.-Dec. selling season could win a form of favored virtual status with the retailer.

Considering the vagueness of the demands and the ambitious deadlines, our sources were properly nonplussed.

"Sounds like category captains all over again," was the wry assessment of one brand marketing executive, who at the time was scrambling to determine whether his company could or should exert itself to meet one grocery chain's timetable.

Adding to the drama of the situation was the looming Year 2000 deadline, roughly concurrent, which demanded the focus of IT experts and budget allocations on both the retailer and supplier sides of the table.

Consultants were called in. Projects were initiated. Upon reflection, most parties came to recognize that the requested time frames were unrealistic for suppliers to the grocery and general merchandise sectors. In the end, common wisdom seems to have prevailed that with few exceptions, retailers must ultimately develop their own online merchandising, selling, and service capability and not rely on their suppliers to build it for them one virtual category at a time.

The mere announcement of a pending "e-business strategy" could trigger stratospheric leaps in a company's market capitalization.

But in their exertions to respond, a number of brand marketers advanced down a path that is leading them this year to confront higher-order e-business objectives. Many had already freed dollars and resources to focus on enterprise-wide technology goals. The e-foundations were being poured that will soon support a robust e-business superstructure.

Strategic Context

At the peak of the dot-com boom, a transactive Web site — that is, a site that can support purchasing transactions — was regarded as something novel and cutting-edge. The mere announcement of a pending "e-business strategy" could trigger stratospheric leaps in a company's market capitalization. Often the "strategy" boiled down to little more than a plan to try to sell something direct to the consumer using a Web site. The company IT whizzes were set to writing code, and interactive agencies were engaged to design some kewl-looking html pages that would dazzle the investment community.

Less than one year later, the mere capability of completing a sale on line is viewed as rather ordinary stuff. Business leaders in all sectors are turning their attention toward using the Web to manage and enhance customer interactions, with the goal of developing stronger and closer business-to-business and business-to-consumer relationships.

For brand marketers, selecting the optimum bundle of software tools to support and enable this broader e-business mandate can be a confusing and slippery process. Good quality choices abound, with nearly all claiming to be the "complete solution" within their own carefully-defined scope.

Where there is already a defined technology goal in place — setting up an online payment processing system, might be one example — there are usually a number of solutions with overlapping capabilities to choose from. Often technical integration considerations will drive the final selection — in other words, you use what works best with what you already have got.

> The times demand a multi-dimensional approach to selecting the tools to enable next generation e-business. An organizing principle is needed.

As a core principle, the business proposition should lead the technology choice — not the other way around. If, for example, the strategy is to develop consumer relationship marketing capabilities, one weighs the desired functionality, software license cost, time to implement, usability and a host of other factors in the decision.

In the rush to get online, a few brand marketers have leaped before looking. They have pushed offerings onto the Web as a reaction to perceived customer demand, stock market trends or competitive pressures without comprehensive due diligence on underlying strategy. Many others have quite sensibly focused their efforts on the Internet as a marketing and advertising medium, dividing their efforts between banner ad programs, "brochureware" corporate Web sites, and delivery of product information such as usage tips or warranty information to consumers.

In short, many brand marketers have reached a kind of inflection point in their e-business life cycles. Many companies are preparing to undertake "next generation" initiatives that go well beyond brochureware or even buying and selling. These higher-order objectives focus on applying Web-based technology to enhance customer loyalty, improve service, streamline business processes, and better manage customer knowledge, skill sets that some in the technology community label customer relationship management, or CRM.

A Holistic Approach

Brand marketers face a twofold realization when it comes to determining their e-business technology needs.

Future success requires a holistic view of organizational direction that goes beyond transactive functionality toward enabling greatly enhanced customer and consumer relationships. And given this context, brand marketers must focus more on the strategic underpinnings of their e-business goals.

In other words, the bar has been raised on technology decisions. The times demand a multi-dimensional approach to selecting the tools to enable next generation e-business. The decisions become unfamiliar and complex. An organizing principle is needed.

A good way to get a firm grip on these issues is to break down the total e-business process into four logical dimensions:

1. **Knowledge Management**, which supports understanding, segmenting and targeting your customers and prospects.
2. **Transactive Management**, which reflects a business model strategy.
3. **Reward Management**, which applies individualized incentives and permission marketing to cement lasting relationships.

4. **Touchpoint Management**, which includes customer care, interaction and relationship strategy.

This four-dimensional taxonomy may help brand marketers to think through the strategic focus that will enable them to reach their e-business goals — profitability, wallet share, market share, higher repeat purchase rates, etc.

The relationship-centric business techniques for pursuing these goals may be similarly parsed into those four categories, as follows:

1. Under the Knowledge heading are such activities as establishing a unified customer information repository, analytic profiling, and predictive modeling.
2. Transactive activities include Internet strategy, order management, e-Commerce transactions, integration with fulfillment and billing systems, among others.
3. The Reward dimension includes permission marketing, targeted one-to-one campaigns, personalized rewards and loyalty programs, and establishing value-added communities.
4. Finally, along the Touchpoint dimension lie such activities as customer contact centers (a.k.a. call centers), assisted selling, customer support, Web self-service, and universal agents (voice, email, chat, fax and voice-over-IP).

With such business activities defined, the next step is to select software. For most of the needs described above, there are a variety of competing tools on the market. Choosing them is not always straightforward, as many claim to be "end-to-end" solutions within universes of their own definition. Features and capabilities tend to overlap as well, as in the case of a Web transaction software package which incorporates some email marketing tools.

Criteria for selection begin with the solutions' features and cost, and extend to their compatibility with your existing enterprise technology and even with each other. There is always the option of developing a proprietary solution, but with so much to master and many choices available, more companies are opting to integrate packaged solutions.

Integration Challenge

Here is where many companies turn to third-party consulting firms for help. While larger brand marketers may possess the technical competencies and staffing depth to tackle e-business development on a multi-dimensional basis, most seek outside assistance to help wrestle the task. But those consultants must be carefully selected and closely managed.

When Forrester Research, Cambridge, Mass., recently reviewed 152 "e-commerce integrators (ECIs)" it selected 40 deemed worth grading. The capabilities studied included strategy, marketing, design and technology.

Of those 40, Forrester reported, none of the ECIs were able to meet all the requirements of a major Web-based project, such as building a procurement system and integrating it with ERP systems and suppliers' sell-side systems.

This implies that the final say in e-business strategy resides with your senior corporate management. The selection of software tools may be influenced by the plans, insights and preferences of departmental leaders from sales, marketing, finance, operations and new business development, as well as from the IT leadership.

Although there is still a lot of work to be done in building out product breadth, security, and leading-edge functionality, the technology enablers for a more advanced approach to Internet commerce are essentially in place. If you can write the check, most second-order e-business skills and capabilities can now be purchased on a more-or-less turnkey basis.

E-business goals have evolved rapidly from online brochures, to simple selling, to advanced customer relationship management.

While online commerce requires certain technology, be assured that decisions in this area are increasingly about core strategy. For most brand marketers, retailers and virtually any company planning to prosper in the 21st century, e-business is no longer a technology project, it's simply business.

Four Dimensions of E-Business

A useful metaphor for depicting the holism in e-business initiatives is based upon a diagram of a human being superimposed upon the points of a compass (with due homage to Leonardo DaVinci):

Transactive management may be visualized as the "feet" of your organization — the buying and selling that are the basic foundation of your enterprise.

Atop this footing are the outstretched arms and hands of your company — touchpoint and reward management — which reflect your firm's capacity to interact with, inform, field customer feedback, and generate loyalty within its customer base.

The head of your organizational "body" is your company's knowledge management — long-term e-business success will be driven by an ability to segment customers, provide customization and personalization on a one-to-many level, and provide value-added content and customer service tailored to the unique needs of individual customers.

Transactive Management: Business Model Strategy

Companies must first form a strategy that details how they want to leverage the Internet. On the Web, firms can inform, buy, sell, distribute, interact, provide support, market, reward, personalize, succeed and fail. Making a determination about business model strategy in the era of the Internet is the most basic cornerstone of success an organization can lay.

Touchpoint Management: Interaction Strategy

Once customers have been attracted, a good relationship marketing strategy will ensure your business is constantly building relationships with these target customers through superior customer service and support. Every interaction a company has with its customers should be personalized and relevant – irrespective of the touchpoint utilized for that interaction.

Reward Management: Incentive Strategy

Those brand marketers able to gain maximum advantage from the Internet must also decide how they will use the Internet to reward good customers. This strategy should detail incentive and loyalty programs they will offer.

Knowledge Management: Targeting Strategy

Brand marketers must analyze customer and market data and use this analysis to devise a strategy to target the most profitable customers.

Five Principles For Selecting E-business Technology

1.

Lead With Strategy, Not Technology — e-business is not an IT project. It is a corporate mandate, which will ultimately permeate your entire business enterprise. Nothing could possibly be more strategic.

2.

Embrace Open Standards — If your goal is to do seamlessly efficient business with multiple retail customers, arriving at a common standard for communications is an evident necessity. That's why the EDI transaction sets were developed during the 90's. For web-enabled business, the UCCnet is an excellent first reference point.

3.

Buy Proven Tools — The adage is correct. Installing version 1.0 of any software may instantly turn your business into a laboratory rat for your software provider. All IT department ego aside, proprietary solutions are often a bad risk — expensive to create and likely to put your overworked tech people on a treadmill of constant upgrades and troubleshooting to remain current. Why not let the software company invest in developing and perfecting feature upgrades?

4.

Get Integration Help — Since any total e-business solution will ultimately require blending together multiple software tools and meeting multiple business objectives, outsourcing is almost always a good idea. Dozens of quality e-Commerce consulting firms are out there competing for your business. Some of the best can provide business strategy consulting and Web design as well as technology implementation and integration.

5.

Don't Burn Bridges — So much has been said about channel conflict that repetition here may seem superfluous, but here goes anyway: For the brand marketer, selling products direct to the consumer may be perceived as a threat to your retail partners' livelihood. Just because the technology is easy to afford and straightforward to install doesn't mean it is prudent to jeopardize multi-million dollar distribution relationships for the sake of a few incremental direct sales.

By summer of 2000, the dot-com startup bubble had clearly burst, with disastrous implications for e-business integrators and born-for-the-Web consulting firms. The following memo was distributed to the Nexgenix, Inc. sales organization on Aug. 20, 2000.

When To Say 'No'

Insights for Business Development Managers

IN OUR UNRELENTING EFFORTS to identify and sign new clients, we regularly encounter opportunities to work with start-up companies and new business initiatives at traditional companies.

While it is certainly desirable to establish relationships with clients as they take their initial steps toward e-business competency, experience has shown us that not all such prospects turn out to be profitable clients.

Part of the BDM's professional responsibility is the *qualification* of new prospects. This is a difficult challenge on its face, and it is made harder by the pressure we place upon ourselves to continually generate new business.

While it is tempting to pursue every lead to conclusion, . Not only are some clients unprofitable, but we suffer an opportunity cost when we devote limited resources toward these clients. We know part of our effort is going to be wasted, but which part?

There is no scientific method for winnowing out the poor business prospects from the good ones, however there are some indicators that may reveal their relative priority.

Following are ten warning signs that may indicate that your "hot prospect" is a risky bet. All of these are based upon actual Nexgenix experiences during the past 12 months:

1. **The Impossible Deadline.** The client is fixated on a near-term deadline, which may be driven by a tactical marketing or sales goal or a demand from a major customer. This situation may be exacerbated by an assumption that timely completion of the Web site is the entire challenge, ignoring an obvious lack of marketing and fulfillment capability.

2. **The Unassailable Business Plan, a.k.a., "Just Build It".** The client presents a competed business plan, based on strategy work done internally or by another consultant. The specifications may or may not be precisely drawn, but the plan is fixed and the company is unwilling to invest in further consultative advice.

As a practical matter, the pursuit of some prospects actually costs us more than they are worth.

3. **Phantom Cash.** The client is a startup, still in the money-raising stages and needs to build a proof of concept or working model site to convince prospective backers that it is "for real." Credit checks reveal a limited pool of available cash, but the client insists that backers are waiting in the wings for some positive news.

4. **Utopian Business Requirements.** The client has drawn up an extremely detailed list of Web site functionalities based on an idealized view of what a perfect site would offer to customers. The concept is brilliant, but the scale of the business opportunity appears unlikely to justify the required investment.

5. **The Mysterious Missing Customer.** The project is led by a technical leader in the client organization, with a mandate from senior management to develop and deploy e-business. But the

company has not thoroughly investigated or considered the marketing justification for the effort. There may not even be a marketing expert involved. Is there a customer for the proposed product or service?

6. **"We're Hiring an E-business VP".** The client is a traditional company planning its first plunge into e-business. It is asking for consultative services leading to a build, but has not yet assigned an executive to take ownership of the effort. The risk? When the new leader is hired, he or she will insist on using resources of his or her own choosing.

7. **Proprietary Hubris.** The client (often experienced in e-commerce) insists on developing a proprietary technical solution to fit its current goals because it is certain, based on past experience, that its Web site embodies a competitive advantage. In some cases the hidden motivation is cost-avoidance or the existence of a large in-house Web development team whose existence must be further justified.

8. **History of Brilliant Failure.** The leadership of the client company has experience with one or more high-profile startups, which generated significant equity in the short term, but never generated actual profits. The latest business concept seems brilliant too, but it defies brief description.

9. **Too Hot to Touch.** The client has successfully raised a pool of venture capital based on a business plan that reflects the absolute latest e-business trend or fad. There's no time for market research. Quality be damned — It's a race to be first to market. Oh and by the way, would your consulting firm accept equity in lieu of cash payment?

10. **Two Years in Development.** The client is a planned startup that seems to have all its ducks in a row — experienced management team, commitment from financial backers and technology allies, years of business concept development. Wait a moment — Could a

business that hasn't got off the ground in two years possibly have missed its window of opportunity? Either the business challenges are too great or the leadership too indecisive.

Wherever possible, Business Development Managers should attempt to identify where these red flags exist, prior to requesting further company resources for pre-sales support.

The presence of one or even several of the above factors may not require that a prospect be automatically excluded from consideration. It may be appropriate to seek counsel with the experts within the vertical consulting practice groups.

The hype surrounding the heavily-funded Internet grocer Webvan engendered a new wave of media and investor interest in the online grocery sector in the Spring of 2000. This column appeared in eRetailing World *in August of that year.*

WILL DEALS BOLSTER ONLINE GROCERY?

I WAS STANDING IN YET ANOTHER AIRPORT CHECK-IN line — destination, San Francisco — when the conversation turned to dot-com retailing. "What about Webvan?" the man asked, mentally reviewing his stock portfolio.

"Good concept, tough location," was my glib response, and I segued into a practiced argument about the importance of route density and how any delivery model is challenged by such physical obstacles as the San Francisco-Oakland Bay Bridge.

"Webvan may find it easier going in Atlanta," I ventured.

My new acquaintance replied that his friend, "one of the first few employees at Webvan," had assured him that the company's high-tech fulfillment facility and order-picking process would power it to lasting competitive advantage.

Sure, I'd heard it before, but I mulled Webvan over for much of the five-hour flight west. Somewhere above the mighty Mississippi, it struck me: The emotion is missing.

For all its cool automation for order assembly; the big contract with Bechtel for a multi-city build-out; the fleets of custom-designed vans; the stream of financial press releases — with all that going on, the Webvan story seems to downplay the human, softer side of the equation.

Call it the other "e" in e-business. When it comes to products we put in, on or near our bodies, like groceries, personal care and household consumables, emotional factors count for a lot.

Between the pixels and the picking, the pioneering online retailers have tended to give short shrift to the consumer relationship.

To be fair, Webvan puts considerable effort into its consumer experience — beginning with a well-designed Web interface and ending with a last-mile delivery formula which is geared toward cultivating a rewarding relationship.

But like its competitors around the country — HomeGrocer, Peapod, Streamline, ShopLink and others — Webvan captures only a subset of each household's consumption. And let's not confuse high switching costs with actual loyalty.

With even their best customers dividing their consumption behavior between store visits and deliveries, can these pure online services cement real emotional connections?

Adding to the challenge, current headlines indicate these e-grocers face a new round of multi-channel competition. America's chain grocery powerhouses are buying in, at distress prices.

At winter's end, the press was forecasting the imminent demise of cash-strapped online grocer Peapod. By the summer solstice, the postman delivered a flyer heralding "Peapod by Stop & Shop," a new service in Connecticut, made possible in large part by Ahold USA's majority investment in the pioneer grocery delivery service. Ahold's multi-chain presence on the East Coast (Bi-Lo, Giant Food, Tops and Edwards) represents a rapid new expansion path for the Peapod service, and its deep-pocketed Dutch parent, Royal Ahold, has the means to fund its rapid integration of the online and offline businesses.

Concurrently, Safeway announced a $10 mm investment in Texas-based GroceryWorks.com, setting up a similar set of alliances with Safeway and its owned chains Tom Thumb, Randall's, Dominick's, and Vons, covering nearly the entire West, Texas and Illinois. Plans are to move swiftly to launch service in those markets.

Meanwhile, Albertson's continued expand and experiment with Albertsons.com in Dallas-Ft. Worth and Seattle.

Because they have the physical presence, branding, and reach to capture the online-offline behavior profile, I believe these large grocery chain operators have a chance to excel where pure dot-com companies like Webvan and ShopLink may struggle.

Large chains didn't invent the idea of e-commerce. They're not even first-movers. But "Internet time" takes on a whole different meaning when you are talking about altering one of the consumer's most fundamental life-organizing behaviors. Purchasing and managing household consumables is a central activity in the art of homemaking. As such it carries great emotional weight.

Between the pixels and the picking, the pioneering online retailers have tended to give short shrift to the consumer relationship. Chain grocers now face an opportunity to step up and take the emotional high ground.

By the first quarter of 2000 traditional retail chains and catalog merchants were confronting the challenges of integrating online sales and services into their existing businesses. The following article appeared in Ideations, *an online publication of the Design Forum, in June 2000.*

TOUCHPOINT INTEGRATION

Challenge for Web Enabled Retailers

WHILE IT IS CERTAINLY DESIRABLE to establish relationships with consumers as they take their initial steps toward e-business competency, experience has shown us that not all such prospects turn out to be profitable.

With the once-stunning innovation of online retailing now a familiar reality, traditional retailers have begun to consider that the virtual store revolution requires a reexamination and reengineering of many of their current business practices.

Many are assimilating online selling skills into their existing businesses. With this innovation comes a new set of business integration challenges, which center around presenting a consistent branding, service and relationship face to shoppers who interact with the retail enterprise at multiple touch points.

As recently as two years ago, dot-com retailers seemed to represent a new and threatening class of trade — an outside threat to the status quo. With stunning speed, however, virtual store selling and online relationship-building have come to be seen as essential new skill sets for any large retail business with designs on a long and successful future.

This shift in perception is increasingly evident at national forums such as the National Retail Federation, International Mass Retailing Association, Direct Marketing Association and Food Marketing Institute trade shows, where traditional retailers currently gather and debate "multi-channel" strategies.

Multi-channel has become a new retail industry code word, which means "add a Web store." Increasingly, major traditional retailers are doing just that. Most are confronting this task as a separate and parallel business project. Fewer are pursuing this mandate with a fully integrated business strategy in hand.

Otherwise sober-minded retail leaders have succumbed to the lure, driven by investor expectations, to launch Web stores based upon less-than-fully-formed business strategies.

Multi-channel retailing is hardly a new concept. It has existed since the glory days of Sears Roebuck, Montgomery Ward and JC Penney, all of which operated catalog businesses alongside their physical store chains throughout most of the last century. The catalogs allowed these retailers to serve customers who were located far away from their stores and they also permitted extended merchandise assortments from a central inventory much broader than any one store could stock.

Broadband Merchants

For today's traditional retailers, the addition of a Web store offers these same benefits. Worth mentioning also is the esteem the announcement of a planned "Web strategy" may win them with the capital markets. More than a few otherwise sober-minded retail leaders have succumbed to this lure, driven by investor expectations to launch Web stores based upon less-than-fully-formed business strategies.

Today, a handful of pioneering thought-leaders, such as Office Depot, Lands End, and Eddie Bauer, offer valuable models for a more integrated business approach. I like to describe them as "broadband merchants" because they have used their online business capabilities to widen their means of contact with the consumer across multiple touch points.

Broadband merchants understand that online selling and consumer relationship management are broadly useful business techniques which cut across existing retail channels. They gear their businesses to recognize each customer every time, regardless of which touchpoint the consumer chooses on a given shopping occasion. They present a consistent branding, merchandising and customer service experience across all touch points and occasions. And they have configured their business processes and systems to support these objectives.

Clearly, the distinction between "multi-channel" and "broadband" business strategy goes beyond mere semantics. It comes down to the difference between "separate and parallel" versus "integrated". The former is a bolt-on, tactical, and finance-driven response to current business realities, while the latter is a much more strategic, visionary, and consumer-centric response to current business conditions.

But broadband merchant synergies extend way beyond the obvious benefits derived from leveraging an established real-world brand into the new virtual marketplace. Web-enabled business practice is an enabler for a whole new level of relationship marketing, which holds the promise to extend, enhance, empower and enable each retailer's customer interactions across multiple consumer touch points.

Brick-and-Mortar Advantage

At the basic level, setting up a functional online storefront appears fairly straightforward. Numerous packaged software solutions are available, and consulting firms will line up to bid on the design and technical work. Compared with the multi-million dollar brick-and mortar new store opening investments some large retailers are used to, building a stand-alone Web store is not even particularly financially intimidating.

Traditional retailers may also enjoy numerous competitive advantages versus their pure-play online competitors. Not the least of these is an existing customer base and consumer brand recognition, assets for which dot-coms must spend lavishly to acquire from scratch. Traditional retailers also possess important distribution infrastructure, merchandising relationships and know-how, financial discipline and access to capital. In the case of catalog merchants, they also may possess significant order-taking and fulfillment capabilities.

Upon examination, however, devising and implementing a sound strategy for leveraging these existing skill sets and assets is not a trivial matter. A multi-channel approach may take advantage of brand recognition and financial resources only, for example, while leaving the Web consumer disconnected from the physical store in terms of merchandising and services.

In contrast, the broadband merchant proposition carries with it the profound implication that the entire retail enterprise must reconfigured to allow for touch point integration. This is serious stuff — no less so than the corporate reengineering efforts which marked the American business landscape in the early 1990s.

Digital Tail — Analog Dog

The broadband merchant model presents both technical and business architecture challenges for the retailer. In order to present a unified branding, service and relationship face to its customers, all its retail touch points must play off a common customer relationship management (CRM) platform. All touch points must access a common pool of customer and merchandising information.

These in turn may play off a set of strategic enablers, such as customer loyalty programs, Web-enabled merchandising software, on-line purchasing solutions, transaction processors, and fulfillment infrastructure. Finally, all of this rides atop a robust extended enterprise technology base.

Described even at this high-level, the broadband merchant architecture implies a reengineering of some core business practices and incorporation of new technologies which many traditional retailers may never have needed before. In some cases, building a robust solution for the Internet implies a changeover of existing store or call center business tools as well.

How is the in-store return of an item purchased on the Web site to be handled, for example? The service policy may be relatively straightforward — satisfy every reasonable customer request. But how is the system to track the movement of that item of merchandise? Will the CRM system adjust the consumer's profile to reflect that the item was returned? Will the value of the return be properly subtracted from the Web store's results and not from the store which provided the service (a matter of great concern to every store manager whose bonus is calculated on sales volume)?

"Broadband" business strategy goes beyond mere semantics. It is a much more strategic, visionary, and consumer-centric response to current business conditions.

This seems to be the point where traditional retail leaders may find themselves facing decision criteria which lie outside their experience. Why, after all, should the modest sales increment anticipated from a virtual storefront justify the total reexamination of a company's tried and true business practices? The investment in technology required to support new broadband business policies may add up to an impressive figure as well.

Here the digital tail may seem to be wagging the analog dog.

Visibility of these issues to senior management may also be compromised if retail leadership delegates the online store development to the status of an information systems department project. While IT professionals should be well qualified to lead the technical development of such a project, the business model, marketing, and customer relationship management strategies require participation from experts in other functional areas of the company.

Often a cross-functional, or task-force approach yields a more complete analysis and more comprehensive strategy for incorporating e-business into the traditional retail enterprise. Outside consultants may be helpful as facilitators.

If incorporating Web technology and e-business practices into a broadband merchant model represents an ultimate goal for a traditional retailer, getting there must begin with carefully chosen steps which lay a robust strategic foundation.

In the end, the decision to integrate e-business practices, technologies, and consumer touch points within a traditional retail business is as much about survival as it is about developing an engine for growth.

Certainly it is about pursuing new sales, but it is also about defending your existing business against new competitors who would chip away at your share of the consumer's wallet. Suddenly, all retailing is e-retailing.

This is the higher ideal: One retailer. One consumer. One e-relationship.

By summer of 2000, the dot-com startup bubble had clearly burst, with disastrous implications for e-business integrators and born-for-the-Web consulting firms. This column appeared in a special supplement to Accessories *and* MR *magazines May/June 2000.*

YOUR DOT-COM RESPONSE: COMPETE, COLLABORATE OR CONSUME?

IN OUR UNRELENTING EFFORTS to identify and sign new clients, we regularly encounter opportunities to work with start-up companies and new business initiatives at traditional companies.

While it is certainly desirable to establish relationships with clients as they take their initial steps toward e-business competency, experience has shown us that not all such prospects turn out to be profitable clients.

Traditional retailers are quickly conquering their initial inability to fully grasp the consequences of the virtual store revolution. Now they face fundamental strategic decisions, which will determine how and if they play in the coming decade.

Many traditional retailers in the apparel and accessories category have prudently watched and waited when it came to pursuing online retailing strategy:

They have sifted the business intelligence from the hype and frenzy.

They have studied virtual retailing technique and prepared methodically in the face of dire warnings about the risk of inaction.

They have resisted the seductive lure of dot-com dollars and focused first on strengthening the bona fide value of their core businesses.

They have observed the metamorphosis of what was initially thought to be a new class of trade into a new business skill set which all retailers must confront and master.

Now two forces are converging on the dot-com scene which may let the conservative, measured response of the traditional retailers be judged as very prudent indeed: A number of prominent dot-com retailers are running low on operating capital. And with the fad-driven venture capital market shifting its focus toward new business-to-business startups, the virtual well may be drying up a bit.

In recent weeks:

CDNow Inc. informed its investors and the public that it may not survive to fulfill its promise as the top music retailer on the Web.

It appears that a number of well-designed but cash-compromised dot-coms are about to line up with their hats in their hands looking for white knights.

Jewelry and luxury retailer Ashford.com announced projected losses of $64 million, up from an estimated $37 million earlier.

Financially challenged online grocer Peapod Inc., down to barely $3 million in operating cash, was rescued by a loan commitment from an unnamed party after a group of investors withdrew $120 million in financing.

BeautyScene.com sold its name and assets to a group of investors, as it had owed a large sum of money to its creditors.

Even some top names are still bleeding cash. Amazon.com, eToys and drugstore.com combined reported net losses of just less than $1 billion last year, according to published reports. (For the record, Amazon's book operation did show a small profit in the fourth quarter of last year.) Other celebrated sites — especially in the online apparel market — have reported marketing spending well in excess of 100% of gross sales, a potentially disastrous formula in which customer acquisition costs far exceed their lifetime value.

Let's be realistic. Players like Amazon.com ($1 billion in the bank) and Webvan ($637 million) have the financial resources to stay in it for the long haul. No doubt a handful of other nimble startups will survive to maturity. But the concentration at the top favors scale and requires real retail skill sets, real investment in brick and mortar assets such as fulfillment centers, and high levels of product and service quality. Only a tiny fraction of 1% of the estimated 700,000 transactive Internet sites possess these capabilities.

This reality may offer a strategic opportunity for the established traditional retailer who is searching for a prudent way to add a virtual retailing face to its sound existing business. For a price tag averaging $30 million or so you can build it yourself using techniques which, thanks to the dot-com startups, are by now fairly well-known.

Or you can take advantage of what to me looks like the sale of the century. It appears that a number of well-designed but cash-compromised dot-coms are about to line up with their hats in their hands looking for white knights.

For the traditional retailer bent on integrating an online consumer interface, the deal opportunities are about to become very attractive. Compete, collaborate or consume, and come out a winner in the bargain.

This VStoreNews *cover story from spring 2000 centered on the notion that leading retailers who successfully melded their online and traditional channels would attain and hold a strong competitive advantage. The term "multichannel retailer" was then coming into vogue. We favor our own coinage.*

BROADBAND MERCHANTS: WHEN ALL RETAILING IS E-RETAILING

Beyond multi-channel retailing lies an even higher ideal: One retailer; one consumer; one e-Relationship

FORGET LOGGING ONTO THE DOT-COMS. For a clear vision of the future of retailing you need only turn on your television. The latest commercial for Office Depot offers a quiet revelation for retailers of all stripes — store-based, Web-based, catalog and direct. "Shop our stores, shop our catalog or shop online," urges the voice-over, above the bouncy jingle, "Taking Care of Business."

The promise of this ad seems so normal, so ordinary, that it's easy to overlook how revolutionary it is within the present retail environment.

With few exceptions, online merchants, traditional retailers and analysts have been unable to move beyond the primitive view of online retailing as a new, competitive channel of trade. But online selling and consumer relationship management are in fact new and broadly useful business techniques, which cut across existing retail channels, and which will change them in fundamental ways.

The inheritors of the future will not be the e-retailing upstarts of the late 1990s. They will be today's visionary traditional retailers, who apply online business technique to establish new and higher standards for customer care atop their already formidable branding and merchandising foundations. Stores will never become extinct. But make no mistake. In a few short years, all retailing will be e-retailing.

The repeated references to something called "multichannel retailing" at this Winter's National Retail Federation convention in New York, suggest there are emerging alternatives to the channel-specific, stovepipe thinking exhibited by the majority of brick-and-mortar and click-to-buy retailers we have observed to date.

"There is very clear evidence that customers don't make a single choice of channels to shop in. We think it's very important to build both channels as one Office Depot," declared David I. Fuente, chairman of the board and CEO of Office Depot, before an NRF audience.

Advised Edward Carey, global director of Deloitte Consulting's consumer business practice in a separate presentation, "Retailers must provide multiple shopping channels, with seamless service across all of those channels."

Clearly these retail thought leaders are thinking in broad terms about the integral way that e-retailing will change traditional business models.

Nevertheless, as widely executed so far by pure dot-coms and even most progressive-minded traditional retailers, the notion of multichannel retailing implies instituting separate and parallel business processes. Witness the unlinked nature of the early Barnes & Noble efforts. Or the surprisingly clumsy attempts by Wal-Mart and Kmart to tackle online selling. Even grocery powerhouse Albertson's has moved sluggishly to integrate its 18-month old online grocery pilot in Dallas-Ft. Worth with its store business, owing perhaps to the sheer magnitude of the fulfillment challenge in that merchandise sector.

But brick-to-click integration is gathering momentum. For the past year or so, *VStoreNews* has been tracking an advanced breed of multi-channel retailers which we label "broadband merchants," because their integrated, Web-enabled business practices allow them to broaden their relationship bandwidth with consumers across multiple touch points.

Broadband Best Practices

Office Depot is among the standout broadband merchants because it has integrated its Internet, catalog, retail store, in-store kiosk, telesales operations, and even its advertising to play off a single version of the merchandising truth. Not far behind is Eddie Bauer, whose smooth linkages between catalog, online and store sales enable a buy-anywhere, return-anywhere customer service that sets a benchmark for the industry.

There are others — 1-800-Flowers, Lands End, J. Crew, KBKids, Nordstrom, Gateway to name a few — which have mastered some key elements of the broadband merchant proposition. Lands End, for example, now inserts a postcard in its recent catalogs which describes how online shoppers may use its "Catalog Quick Order" feature by entering the printed item numbers in a space on the site's home page.

> Clearly these retail thought leaders are thinking in broad terms about the integral way that e-retailing will change traditional business models.

A bit farther down the broadband merchant continuum is Toys "R" Us, which is certainly multi-channel, but which has only partially linked its store and online businesses. The company progressed this year with its policy of accepting returns of goods purchased on line in its stores, but it has a way to go. A harbinger of further online-in store integration, however, is evident on a recent Toys "R" Us ad circular, which urges shoppers to look for a tiny icon of a computer below each listed items alongside its "online item number" to facilitate easy online ordering.

The Lands End and the Toys "R" Us innovations suggest a unification trend within the merchandising strategies of each company. While the total offerings in the store or catalog and on line may not be identical in scope or specifics, clearly these companies are viewing their assortments through a single lens. The result is a more consistent presentation to the consumer — a first step in quality customer care.

On the consumer relationship side, Lands End is the more successful of the two. Here the company's catalog experience is an asset, for it can recognize a returning shopper via a phone, fax, catalog or Internet order. Toys "R" Us at present has no visible means for observing, much less measuring the total value of a customer relationship.

Admittedly, seamless integration of branding, merchandising, service and relationships across multiple consumer touch points is a considerable feat, but we can anticipate that such capability will be the price of entry in the retail competition of the next few years.

In the future of "multichannel retailing," Ed Carey of Deloitte predicted, "Consumer expectations will raise the bar for all retailers. They will expect 24 x 7 availability; rich product information and offerings; sharp pricing; and an easy shopping experience."

"E-Engineering" The Corporation

True broadband merchants understand how online retailing and its associated e-business tools present a great opportunity for retailers to encourage, enhance and expand their customer relationships. For retailers who persist in separating their virtual and physical retailing operations, the penalty will be discontinuity in their consumer relationships — a perceived lower level of service — resulting in competitive disadvantage.

That's why Paul Hoedeman, vice president information services of The Home Depot expressed this sentiment at the NRF: "We are not going to have a separate, stand-alone Internet strategy," he stated. "It's going to be integrated into our business."

Broadband merchants clearly will leverage a clear advantage in branding, continuity across multiple consumer touch points, and ultimately in establishing and maintaining what the industry is beginning to call "e-Relationships."

Hoedeman added a few more advantages to this list. "All our stores are warehouses and we have a great delivery infrastructure," he said. "Every day we do more volume delivery than Amazon.com — and we make money at it. We've tried and tested in ways the dot-coms have never even imagined."

Talk about leveraging the inherent advantages of an entrenched traditional retailer. Can the venture capital-backed dot-coms, most of whom have barely progressed past the decision to spend half their cash on Super Bowl ads, ever hope to match these skills before their investors run out of patience?

Broadband Pioneers

So it seems the distinction we now obsess over — between click-to-buy and brick-and-mortar merchants — certainly seems profound in the present moment, but will soon be revealed as trivial.

For successful merchants and their suppliers, Web-enabled merchandising, selling, consumer relationships and supply-chain operations will permeate business practices in the next decade. The pioneers described on these pages are merely the first to attempt to develop new best practices for the new millennium.

They seek to present an integrated merchandising and brand personality. They seek to recognize each customer regardless of which channel he or she chooses to use on a given occasion. They seek to serve the customer whenever and wherever and however the customer demands to be served.

They are the first broadband merchants. But not the last.

Our spring 2000 edition of VStoreNews *embodied two firsts, both thanks to the backing of our patrons at Nexgenix. The issue was printed in rich color on luxurious paper stock and it was distributed by post to more than 10,000 retail executives. I found the parallels between broadband publishing and broadband retailing intriguing, and told our readers why in this column.*

PULP! (NOT FICTION)

VSN WORLD HEADQUARTERS, WESTPORT, CT — What's this you're reading? A paper edition of *Virtual Store News*? The elite group of "thought leaders" who had been exposed to *VStoreNews* and *VSN TopLine* by email, Web or fax since we created it in 1998 are now being joined by thousands of new retailing, brand marketing and business technology leaders, who will receive it by post. If you're one of our new readers, welcome. If you are an old friend, welcome back.

For a purely virtual business like *VStoreNews*, the shift to a print format may be perceived as retro-radical. After all, who moves an e-Business from bits to pulp? Well, for one, the e-zine *Wired* did, and that's not bad company. Inversely, increasing numbers of print publications are folding in electronic editions. The idea is to serve each reader, at each moment, in the ways each prefers to be served.

VStoreNews has been reconfigured to match this new paradigm — what I'd like to call "broadband publishing." It combines this printed journal with an informational web site, http://VStoreNews.com, and our biweekly email bulletin, *VSN TopLine*. One knowledge business — multiple channels for users to interact with the content.

This broadband publishing proposition bears more than a metaphoric parallel with the broadband retailing trend that we cover in this edition of *VStoreNews*. Our new multi-format mirrors a world where broadband merchants widen business models to permit consumers to interact seamlessly with their businesses through a variety of channels — stores, Web sites, kiosks, catalogs, telesales, and good old-fashioned human-to-human contact.

Make no mistake, the V in *VStoreNews* still stands for Virtual. Coverage of strategy, analysis and opinion about Web-enabled retailing is still our *raison d'être.* Fascinating how, at least for the contents of this issue, form follows nonfiction.

Let's be crystal clear: What I call broadband publishing or broadband business of any kind is not predicated on what the telecommunications, advertising and broadcasting industries calls broadband Internet. The latter is about technology — building a wider electronic "pipe" which permits real-time transmission of rich content over the Internet, such as interactive advertising, full-motion video and other forms of messaging and entertainment.

Broadband merchants take deliberate and dramatic steps to integrate the retail business across all its consumer touch points. One business. One customer. One relationship. Everywhere.

Why then do I insist on describing as "broadband merchants" what others in this industry prefer to tag as "multichannel retailers"?

Two reasons. First, multichannel retailing implies separate but parallel transactional capabilities. Broadband merchants take deliberate and dramatic steps to integrate the retail business across all its consumer touch points. One business. One customer. One relationship. Everywhere.

The second reason is about branding. Broadband merchants represent the next step in a continuum of retail development. To identify and discuss a trend you have to assign it a label. So we branded it, self-consciously, to distinguish this new trend from those which preceded it.

While the broadband merchant proposition is about what happens in stores and catalogs too, it requires Internet technology to be realized. It's the connectivity that counts, backed by the business intelligence to cultivate a truly broadband customer relationship.

Will broadband retailers use broadband technology? Absolutely. Streaming media, voice-over-IP telephony, three-dimensional imagery and increasingly dynamic Web-services are all lurking in our digital commerce future. But it's not the size of the image file that really counts, it's what you do with the relationship.

My Advice?

Keep broadening your business bandwidth. But keep hold on the one truth that matters: Earn, re-earn, and re-re-earn each customer relationship at every touch point, every time.

A national debate has swelled and ebbed over the question of whether or not to require online shoppers to pay sales tax on their purchases. The matter has some strong political undertones and yet many politicians have avoided taking a strong stand. When the two major party candidates in the 2000 Presidential race were selected, they were each on record as to their positions on this tricky topic. As things turned out, both successfully ducked this issue in the election, leaving it as a future headache for the lucky winner.

THE ART OF 'POLITAX'

THE INTERNET SALES TAX BATTLE has finally made the big time. When the national advisory commission established by Congress 14 months ago to explore the issue convened again in Dallas on March 20, the venerable *New York Times* saw fit to preview the event as the lead story on its business section.

A decision will be required in short order about whether to extend or to end the current moratorium on sales tax for online purchases. But as reporter David Cay Johnston observed, the commission "will almost certainly fail to reach a consensus about what national policy to recommend."

Now the two sides are lined up eyeball-to-eyeball. On the right, so to speak, are mostly anti-big government Republican senators and representatives who chant the "no new taxes" refrain. On the left are Governors and municipal leaders, worried that their traditional revenue source is being leached away, calling for a "level playing field," in which all consumer purchases are taxed, regardless of the channel in which they are made.

In an interesting reversal of this line-up, Republican presidential candidate, Governor George W. Bush avows sympathy for the phrase made immortal by his father after the famous, "read my lips." Meanwhile, Democratic candidate Vice President Al Gore has stood up for the level playing field principle.

Eerily quiet in this debate over public policy to date have been the major retail trade associations, such as the National Retail Federation, the National Mass Retail Institute and the Food Marketing Institute, which represent department and specialty stores, discounters and mass merchants, and grocery stores respectively. The two former groups finally made their first position statements in favor of the level playing field this Winter, more than a year after the commission's ruling, and more than two years after the U.S. Department of Commerce held public hearings on the topic.

New competitors will soon offer cheap, fast Web site plug-ins that seamlessly handle the calculation, collection and payment of sales tax to all 350 municipal jurisdictions.

A few observations about the current sales tax moratorium:

One: It's regressive. Since Internet access is a privilege available primarily to computer owners and to people who use Web-enabled PCs in their jobs, a whole cadre of Americans — lower middle class and working poor — have not enjoyed access to the online tax dodge.

Two: Due to the abdication by the traditional retail community, the current policy has been influenced primarily by companies in the telecommunications and dot-com world, not by the retailers and brand marketers whose interests are most deeply affected.

Three: This debate is troubling news for the traditional direct marketing and catalog sales industry, which has enjoyed a free ride for many years with respect to not charging sales tax to its out-of-state customers. Sorry guys, a level playing field will include you too.

Four: The only righteous principle for determining which sales tax calculation to use for a purchase is that the law of the ship-to address must apply. Any other scheme will cause all the online retailers and catalogers to relocate to the Cayman Islands.

The number one myth in the dot-tax debate is the shameful assertion that the task of collecting the sales tax will be unfairly onerous for the many small dot-com operators. To this we offer the following rebuttal: Considering the pace of innovation in software development today, how long would it take for ten new competitors to arise offering cheap, fast Web site plug-ins that seamlessly handle the calculation, collection and payment of sales tax to all 350 municipal jurisdictions?

Sounds like a dot-com opportunity in the making.

By spring of 2000, I was using every opportunity to drive forward the broadband merchant terminology, despite the growing popularity of the phrase, "multichannel retailer." The following column appeared in Chain Store Age *in March 2000.*

BEYOND MULTICHANNEL RETAIL

Broadband merchants enjoy expanded consumer relationships

REMARKABLY, MUCH OF THE BUZZ at this year's National Retail Federation convention in New York was focused on an old idea turned new again — "multichannel retailing."

I say remarkably, because at the same event just one year earlier, the mere idea that mainstream retailers should acquire the skills to merchandise and transact sales on the Internet seemed downright revolutionary. Now the smart money is saying that virtual store selling and online relationship-building are destined to become core skill sets for (formerly) traditional retailers.

How has our notoriously conservative industry moved so fast and so far? Part of the answer, I think, is that the apparent rate of progress is partly virtual. In truth, a year ago many traditional retailers were much farther along on e-retailing than they were letting on.

For validation, examine the Shop.org/Boston Consulting Group industry survey released last winter, which indicated that in 1998, three-fifths of online consumer dollar sales were captured by so-called traditional retailers.

The pure dot-coms, for all their hype and market capitalization, controlled but a minority of online dollars.

This result seemed counterintuitive. But upon examination, it could be at least partly explained by the early and aggressive moves by traditional catalog companies to the Internet. Brick and mortar chains moved a bit more slowly but, according to the Ernst & Young survey released at last year's NRF, a strong majority of those retailers reported plans to be selling online by the end of 1999.

In a way, this season's buzz phrase, multi-channel retailing, is really as old as Sears & Roebuck, JC Penney and Montgomery Ward, all of which ran strong catalog sales operations in parallel with their retail stores for much of the prior century. One might say this is an idea whose time had already come. What's remarkable is how relevant it is becoming again in the present Internet-empowered business environment.

For the past year or so, I've been tracking an advanced breed of multi-channel retailers which I label "broadband merchants," because their integrated, Web-enabled business practices allow them to broaden their relationship bandwidth with consumers across multiple touch points.

In truth, a year ago many traditional retailers were much farther along on e-retailing than they were letting on.

Among my favorite broadband merchants is Office Depot, which has integrated its Internet, catalog, retail store, in-store kiosk, and telesales operations to play off a single version of the merchandising truth. Not far behind is Eddie Bauer, whose smooth linkages between catalog, online and store sales enable a buy-anywhere, return-anywhere customer service that sets a benchmark for the industry. There are others — 1-800-Flowers, Lands End, J. Crew, Nordstrom, Gateway — which have mastered some elements of the broadband merchant proposition.

On the further end of the broadband merchant continuum are merchants like Toys "R" Us, which is certainly multi-channel, but which has not yet unified its store and online businesses. The company progressed this year with its policy of accepting returns of goods purchased on line in its stores, but it has a way to go.

Admittedly, seamless integration of branding, merchandising, service and relationships across multiple consumer touch points is a considerable feat, but we can anticipate that such capability will be the price of entry in the retail competition of the next few years.

Broadband merchants understand how online retailing and its associated e-business tools present a great opportunity for retailers to encourage, enhance and expand their customer relationships. For retailers who persist in separating their virtual and physical retailing operations, the penalty will be discontinuity in their consumer relationships — a perceived lower level of service — resulting in competitive disadvantage.

Broadband merchants possess a clear edge in branding, continuity across multiple consumer touch points, and ultimately in establishing and maintaining what the industry is beginning to call "e-relationships."

When RT *magazine timed its metamorphosis into* RetailTech *to coincide with the Year 2000 excitement, I was one of the lucky ones selected to offer a forward-looking essay for the Millennium. My colleagues in this undertaking were all highly accomplished, but none shone in my estimation as brightly as The Amazing Kreskin, famed de-bunker of charlatans and a friend of* RT *editor Bruce Fox. I remain deeply honored to this day that my photograph appeared with Kreskin's on the cover of the January 2000 issue.*

ALL RETAILING IS ERETAILING

THE DISTINCTION WE NOW OBSESS OVER — between click-to-buy and brick-and-mortar merchants — certainly seems profound in the present moment, but will soon be revealed as trivial. Here's an alternate perspective:

Most observers continue to regard e-retailing as new channel for bringing products to the consumer market. But online selling is in fact a new and fundamental business technique, which cuts across existing retail channels. For successful merchants and their suppliers, Web-enabled merchandising, selling, consumer relationships and supply-chain operations will permeate business practices in the next decade.

This outlook is in no way limited to the so-called "pure-play" virtual stores, which have made so many headlines with their audacious forays into the consumer marketplace. Within 10 years there will be virtually no retail consumer selling in this country that does not incorporate Web-enabled business practice.

For traditional retailers, this means the adoption of e-retailing as an extension and enhancement of their ability to meet consumer needs and expectations. Here, the power of the Web as a dynamic, responsive medium of interaction will motivate profound and discontinuous changes throughout the retail enterprise. Ultimately this skill set will enable unprecedented levels of customer service and relationship building.

Traditional retailers who incorporate online selling are sometimes labeled "multi-channel." I prefer to describe them as "Broadband Merchants," because the addition of the communications power of the Web allows the retailer to "broaden its bandwidth" with respect to its customer relationships.

Here's my definition of broadband merchants:

- They simultaneously leverage stores, the Internet, Web kiosks, telesales, catalog, fax, TV, etc. to extend, enhance and empower their retail enterprise.
- They maintain a unified, consistent branding proposition across all of their sales, media and advertising activities.
- They maintain a robust, flexible and seamless enterprise-wide technology base, which supports all consumer interactions.
- They are prepared to sell goods and services in any and every way that the consumer wants to buy.

The addition of the communications power of the Web allows the retailer to "broaden its bandwidth" with respect to its customer relationships.

The Broadband Merchant principle implies that while the *transaction* may seem like the whole trick to today's virtual retailers, the real opportunity lies in the *interaction* — the attraction, cultivation and retention of customers over time.

Nowhere does this imply — in contrast with the claims now being made by dot-com retailers — that "customer acquisition" is somehow the primary goal. Attracting the initial transaction may be a desperate need for retailers that have no customers, but Broadband Merchants will focus on maximizing the lifetime value of their customers by continually proving and re-proving the beneficial value of the relationship with every interaction, online and in the store.

We are witnessing the emergence of a new kind of online goods and services provider: It offers interactive choices to consumers. It respects the consumers' ultimate ownership of the relationship. It uses web-enabled business processes to organize its offering around the unique and individualized needs of each consumer.

When all is said and done, retailing will remain retailing. The core values of trust, service, fair dealing and competitive prices will remain the pillars of any consumer-merchant relationship.

With the turn of the Millennium, the Great Divide which so many of us assume now separates online retailing from traditional retailing will blur and disappear. In its wake, Broadband Merchants will emerge, for whom all retailing is e-retailing.

The final installment of VSN TopLine *focused once again on the goings on in the online grocery sector. At the time, Albertson's was threatening to become the 800-pound gorilla of multi-channel grocery retailing. We shined a little light on them.*

ALBERTSON'S WEIGHS IN — AGAIN

VSN TopLine — Dec. 15, 1999

NOW THAT EVERY OTHER major bricks-and-mortar retail category has moved online, it's about time for the historically slow-to-change grocery trade to get serious about this dot-com business. And sure enough, Albertson's — the Boise, Idaho-based company that is the nation's second-largest grocery chain — has signaled its intention to do so with a 31,000-square-foot hybrid Internet fulfillment center and supermarket operation in the Seattle suburb of Bellevue, Washington.

The prototype clicks-and-mortar store is about half the size of Albertson's regular stores. It allows customers to either roll real carts down real aisles between real gondolas of real food — or stop by a computer terminal in the store and order their groceries for delivery within an hour and a half, or sometime later. (Why consumers would stop by this physical store instead of ordering from the comfort of their own dens, the company didn't say.)

Albertson's believes that whatever trouble it's going to in order to make the concept work in Bellevue, and presumably elsewhere in the U.S., is worth it to make its presence felt in the online market. Unlike its pure dot-com rivals, the company already has an infrastructure in place for procuring, storing, distributing and marketing groceries, notes Patrick Steele, an Albertson's executive.

All of this generated considerable excitement, of course. Albertson's is trying to outpace competing mega-chains like Safeway Inc., which has been learning from the collaborative business model it operates with online-grocer Peapod Inc., which is based in Chicago. Not to mention all the dot-com companies that have been hacking away at the Internet-grocery business for a couple of years now, including not only Peapod but also, Boston-based Streamline, Foster City, Calif.-based Webvan Group Inc. and Kirkland, Wash.-based Home Grocer.

And, in fact, Bellevue is Albertson's second market for e-commerce — its first is a little-discussed project in Dallas-Ft. Worth that is more than 15 months old. And the company also recently announced an online retailing strategy for its Sav-On drug-store chain in test markets in Kansas City and Las Vegas.

Lest you are convinced that Albertson's interest in online retailing is newly founded, consider this seldom-told tale: The company is said to have made acquisition overtures to Peapod a couple of years back, invited the management team in and studied the business model intensely before a change of heart. A half-year later, Albertson's launched its test in DFW.

(Author's note: Freelance writer Dale Buss contributed to this essay.)

Marketers of consumer products need to confront e-business too. The distraction of the looming 'Y2K crisis' limited most brand marketers to the status of spectator to the dot-com revolution. But aggressive grocery chains continued to test the limits of their suppliers' willingness to provide value-added services. This column appeared in Brand Marketing *magazine in December 1999.*

NEXT Y2K CHALLENGE: PACKAGING E-SOLUTIONS

"SOUNDS LIKE CATEGORY CAPTAINS all over again," a business development executive for a major branded grocery manufacturer told me recently.

"They are requiring a presentation from us by year-end," said the national sales manager for a major grocery distribution company.

"We have been getting requests from numerous accounts," agreed the consumer direct manager of a large consumer products company.

These brand marketers share a common concern: Supermarket chains are asking their suppliers to bring them solutions for e-retailing in their product categories.

Online merchandising is shaping up to be a major trade relations challenge for the year 2000. How is a manufacturer to respond?

There is no easy answer. Most manufacturers of fast-moving consumer goods have already concluded, quite correctly, that they should not pursue the business of selling their products direct to the consumer using the

Internet. Better, they reason, to avoid channel conflict and let retailers assume the traditional role of value-added intermediary online.

For the most part, however, major grocery chains have moved sluggishly to extend their franchises onto the Web. Generally they have pursued top-line growth by more familiar means, such as the corporate acquisitions which have occupied the attention of Kroger, Albertson's and Ahold USA this year. On the technology front, most chains have been preoccupied with resolving the Y2K bug, leaving little time to confront dot-com strategies.

This has left most of the online grocery initiative to pure-play Internet grocers such as Webvan, HomeGrocer.com, and Peapod and to a handful of innovative regional chains such as Basha's. Overall online sales penetration in this sector remains low, at less 0.1 % of total U.S. sales by one recent estimate. This leaves enormous opportunity on the table for chain grocers, and they want help from their suppliers.

Without exception, the brand marketers who discussed this development with me said they were eager to be of service. Prior experiences in trade relations, category management, solution selling and ECR have taught manufacturers that collaboration with retailers is often good business.

The same experiences, however, suggest that some of these requests for e-retailing solutions might be cost-shifting attempts. Brand marketers should seek to treat this new dialog as an opportunity for strategic collaboration, and not allow it to become merely a new form of trade allowance.

There is no roadmap available for this conversation yet, no recognized best practice to fall back on. Conscientious manufacturers will try to help their customers think broadly about their e-retailing opportunity, rather than focusing on á la carte tactical implementation within each category.

In 1999 VStoreNews *began releasing a series of free email briefings commenting on current industry events. This installment was among the best received, generating much reader feedback and a handful of interview requests from newspaper reporters.*

LEVI'S CUTS E-PANTS SHORT

VSN TopLine — Nov. 3, 1999

ONE WONDERS HOW PAINFUL the inevitable retailer backlash had become. Levi Strauss was a pioneer among manufacturers seeking to bring branded goods direct to the consumer over the Internet beginning in November of 1998. Now comes word that the company will back away from that strategy by year-end, allowing its retail partners to do the selling instead.

The San Francisco-based company, which has been operating transactional sites for both its Levi's and Dockers lines of casual clothing, said two of its largest retail customers, JC Penney and Macy's, would begin selling its products on their web sites after the holidays.

Levi's public explanation for this turnabout is the unsustainable high-cost of operating a "world-class e-commerce business." We think channel conflict might be more candid explanation.

For consumer product manufacturers, strategically powerful distribution depends upon favorable relationships with the retail trade. Selling your products on line in competition with your best customers is probably not the best way to curry favor with them and win in-store support for your brands.

In fact, it's a pretty good way to get your trade marketing kneecaps broken, figuratively speaking.

The arrival last month of new Levi Strauss CEO Philip Marineau lends an underscore to this interpretation. The former PepsiCo, Dean Foods and Quaker Oats executive has a long track record in the packaged goods arena. As his greatest past achievement — with Quaker's Gatorade brand — would suggest, Marineau understands the crucial role of a strong distribution system to a brand's success.

It seems, after all, that branded product manufacturers really can't have it both ways. In theory a strong-enough brand should be able to choose the consumer-direct route with impunity, leaving retailers with no choice but to grin and bear it. But today's largest retailers are in many ways more powerful than the brand marketers, and they have many choices of branded product to sell, online and offline.

Levi Strauss has tested its considerable brand power in this arena and is now backing down. In its experience lies a sobering message for other brands that are being seduced toward disintermediation by the dot-com frenzy.

The following editor's note accompanied this edition of VSN TopLine*: "Welcome to the Inaugural Issue of* VSN TopLine, *the free weekly email bulletin from the editors of* VStoreNews®. *Each week we focus on analysis of one key current event from the world of online retailing and marketing. You receive a concise point of view direct to your email, complete with relevant links to hard news stories."*

zSHOPS MEET VSTORES — AND MORE

VSN TopLine — Oct. 6, 1999

VIRTUAL MEGA-RETAILER Amazon.com is proposing to do for online retailing what online community sites like Geocities, iVillage and Tripod have done for personal home pages.

Its new "zShops" service lets retailers, small and large, build their own online shops, using Web-based tools. Amazon provides the merchandise assortment, order fulfillment and even offers credit-card clearing as an optional service. For the modest sum of $9.99 a month, plus a percentage of each sale, would-be Web merchants can list up to 3,000 items on "zShops," the area on Amazon's site devoted to the sellers. Amazon.com offers a selection of several hundred thousand items which zShop proprietors may "stock" on their "zShelves."

But Amazon is hardly the only company working to bring the concept of template-driven, do-it-yourself merchandising to the Web. In fact, it's not even the first.

Vstore.com, actually a two-year old web site founded by Scottsdale, AZ entrepreneur Dan Kennedy, launched a very similar service earlier this summer, which allows consumers to establish virtual stores which purvey merchandise from a comprehensive offering provided through a proprietary "Storefront Wizard". Vstore operators pay only commissions on the sales. (Note: Vstore.com and VStoreNews have absolutely no affiliation or business ties.)

Now preparing for an October 18 launch is StoreRunner.com, which will leverage a reported $100 million commitment from CBS/Viacom. The web site is actually already operative, and it describes a simple process whereby existing merchants or new Web-entrepreneurs can use web links and/or "micro-sites" to offer products for sale. The product offerings are indexed on the site, which permits online shoppers to search and compare them and complete their purchases.

Another interesting, if less well-funded, player is Summit Payment Solutions. Founded by a group of former New England banking and real estate executives, it has built a Web-based service offering aimed at small independent retailers who need both online merchandising help and transaction processing. Participants' stores are aggregated into directory of online catalogs, which consumers browse through.

Amazon's entry into this emerging DIY merchandising sector will surely focus interest on the idea that anyone with a browser and a dream can be a Web merchant. But these stores aren't designed to scale up easily and it's hard to predict whether, even in aggregate, they will account for a significant slice of the online retailing pie.

TENSER'S TIRADES

I was getting fed up with some of the glib rhetoric being spouted by the pocket-protector crowd out in the Silicon Valley. One of the most unfortunate concepts, in my humble opinion, was the notion that successful Web sites had a characteristic called "stickiness." The following Tirade appeared in the September, 1999 edition of VStoreNews.

TAKE YOUR WEB PORTAL AND STICK IT!

VSN WORLD HEADQUARTERS, WESTPORT, CT — Somebody explain to me again how "stickiness" is a good thing? Sorry, I just don't get it.

I mean, how is the *consumer* served by a Web site that's designed to prevent visitors from leaving? The point of having an Internet (I've read and been told so many times that I believe it), is to promote communications and to make information quickly and efficiently available to everyone. You've got questions; the Web's got 10 billion answers.

That was the beauty of the original "search engines." The developers of Alta Vista, Yahoo! and Excite set their 'bots to crawl all over the World Wide Web indexing and cataloging sites, so that hapless, Mosaic-browsing, 14.4 modem-using Internauts like myself could actually locate things of interest before our shaky dial-up connections timed out.

Best of all, it was all free! The prevailing ethic of the time held that Web content was accessible to all, ownable by none. The mere whiff of commercial speech set the cyber-libertarians a-flamin' the online bulletin boards. Search engines were immediately popular because they *saved time.* They added value to the Web-surfing experience.

Well that was back in the dim mists of Web history — about 1995 — when content was supposedly king. This business has apparently wised up since then. In the past two years the search engines have given way to "portals," vast, multi-purpose web sites whose stated purpose is the gathering of vast quantities of eyeballs into a mass audience that has an attraction to advertisers.

While this model has some serious flaws, we must concede that media advertising has been an important driver of continued commercial development on the World Wide Web. The sale of online content is profitable for only a tiny number of sites. Many "dot-com" business plans cite advertising revenues as a primary source of revenues — and that includes a good number of Vstores.

The trouble is that once you focus a Web site on maximizing value for your advertisers (and by extension, your venture capital backers), the consumer proposition winds up taking the back seat. Instead of helping you get *elsewhere* quickly and efficiently, the portals devise ways of keeping you *here,* so their advertisers (who usually pay in proportion to page views and/or click-throughs) stand a better chance of accumulating lots of viewers.

The nature of the Web-surfing experience (lean forward, assertively select and interact with the content) is the inverse of television (sit back, absorb content passively).

How did the model get inverted? It stems, I think, from the wishful application of mass-media advertising models to a medium that is the opposite of mass. The nature of the Web-surfing experience (lean forward, assertively select and interact with the content) is the inverse of television (sit back, absorb content passively). The only similarity is the glowing screen.

Mass models don't apply. Individualized message delivery is the real promise of the Internet. Give me relevance or give me death! And don't clutter up my Web experience with excess services and don't slow my already snail-like download times with rich-media banners and pop-ups that were designed with one objective in mind: To convince the advertiser that his online media spending is justified.

The good news is that these revelations are not lost on many industry leaders.

"We as an industry have done a bad job in allowing the term 'stickiness' to proliferate. It's really about relevance and utility," said Charles Moldow, vice president of sales and marketing for @Home Network at the Harvard Business School Cyberposium '99.

"No one ever really gets stuck in the Internet. Sometimes the best thing for us to do is pass the person along to elsewhere," said David Risher, senior vice president of Amazon.com, at the same parley. "It would be shortsighted to think only of keeping people on your site. This is a balance."

Well stated, gentlemen. The bloated portals are coming to a moment of destiny as many of their high-priced advertiser deals come up for renewal this year. The bean counters are licking their pencils and calculating their ROIs. Yahoo!, Excite, et al, are all rushing to expand their online shopping centers, in the hope that longer online times and sales commissions will offset the inevitable flattening of ad rates.

From this cranky surfer's perspective, a sticky web site has all the appeal of a glob of bubble gum on your shoe.

My Advice?

Un-stick your thinking. Put the consumer first.

My former university classmate Jay Walker was briefly one of the richest men in America on the strength of his astonishing early success with Priceline.com. (Alas, that level of success proved fleeting.) When he announced a leap into grocery promotion I felt compelled to offer a critique. The following commentary appeared in the September, 1999 VStoreNews.

In WebHouse Club, Priceline Invokes a Namesake

IS THERE A MYSTICAL LINK between the Price/Costco membership warehouse chain and Priceline.com's "Name Your Own Price" brand of online retailing?

Priceline.com chairman Jay Walker certainly tried to invoke the spirit of retailing pioneer Sol Price when he announced the planned launch of the new WebHouse Club online service before the Grocery Manufacturers of America Internet Marketing & Promotions Seminar here on Sept. 21.

Maybe the link is more linguistical than mystical. Sol Price may well have been the most fortuitously-moniker'd retail executive ever. Twenty-five years ago he transformed retailing by changing the cost-of-selling rules, lowering gross margins, and charging Price Club shoppers an up-front membership fee for the privilege of pushing flat-bed carts around a concrete floor.

Now Walker, who is worth several $billions in equity as a result of his success with Priceline.com, is proposing to "reinvent retailing" on new terms. The Priceline WebHouse Club, a new privately-held company, will allow registered customers to "name their own price" for common grocery products over the Internet, pre-pay for them at discounted prices, then pick them up at local grocery stores. (A link to the WebHouse Club home page is accessible from www.priceline.com.)

But is it really retailing that Walker is reinventing? Based on his description and the few web pages that can be seen, WebHouse Club feels more like an online vehicle for delivering manufacturer-funded deals to consumers than a vehicle for selling goods.

WebHouse Club will be operated as a separate corporate entity, allied with Priceline.com. Both employ the patented "name your own price" business process, licensed by Walker's technology development firm, Walker Digital.

Set for a Nov. 1 launch in metropolitan New York, the program has already signed up 600 participating chain retail outlets operated by ShopRite, King Kullen, A&P, Waldbaum's, D'Agostino, Gristede's and others. He aggressively forecast 25,000 participating stores nationwide within 15 months.

Whoever claimed that profit levels would be higher on the Web because its consumers are less price-sensitive was looking at a very narrow consumer group, to say the least.

Walker, who clearly enjoys the podium, shrewdly chose the GMA forum for this announcement. The audience was populated by senior executives from Procter & Gamble, Nabisco, McNeil Consumer Healthcare, Ralston Purina and Nestle, among others, who had gathered in Manhattan for a day-long briefing on Internet marketing.

The WebHouse Club announcement was apparently unsettling to some manufacturers in the room, if for no other reason than Walker's continual repetition of the mantra of Price/price. You could read margin erosion in their eyes. The concept apparently depends upon manufacturers to fund the discounts, which can range as high as 50% off normal retails.

Is this for real? One indication may lie in the assembly of seasoned retail talent on board: President and CEO Jon Otto was the former founder and owner of RockBottom, a deep-discount drug store chain. Head of merchandising Rob Voss was the man selected by Wal-Mart founder Sam Walton to found Sam's Wholesale Club.

Another indication may be the $65 million in initial venture financing expected from Walker Digital, Wit Capital, Vulcan Ventures, Goldman Sachs and several other private investors. A third may be the $25 million planned ad campaign starring actor William Shatner.

The message for grocery retailers and their suppliers is that this novel concept must be taken seriously, even if its business concepts seem far outside the box.

Like the Price Club 25 years ago, WebHouse Club is aimed toward driving down consumer prices. Manufacturer margins may go along with them. Whoever claimed that profit levels would be higher on the Web because its consumers are less price sensitive was looking at a very narrow consumer group, to say the least.

As Jay Walker put it, "Time is only more important than money for people who have no time and lots of money." The late Sol Price was probably cheering him on from retail heaven.

The acquisition of pioneering online drugstore Soma.com by the CVS drugstore chain set off a chain reaction in the sector that was a harbinger of events to come. The following column appeared in RT *magazine in July 1999.*

ESTABLISHED DRUG MERCHANTS: VIRTUALLY UNSTOPPABLE

WEB-ONLY MERCHANTS TAKE NOTE: The heavy-hitters of the chain drug industry are taking some serious swings at the World Wide Web.

The announcement on May 17 that CVS will pay $30 million to acquire 6-month-old virtual druggist Soma.com marks a major milestone for chain retailing. CVS is the first major drug store chain to broaden its consumer bandwidth in this manner, but it will almost certainly not be the last.

While the efforts to date by other top chains appear mainly defensive and limited to prescription refills, Walgreens, Rite Aid, J C Penney and Wal-Mart are also capable of emerging as online drugstore leaders.

This prediction may not warm the hearts of the brave visionaries behind Drugstore.com, PlanetRx and their kin, but even well-funded Silicon Valley startups and IPOs are obligated to accept reality as it is, not as they envision it to become in their .COM business plans.

Selling prescription drugs and personal care items on the Internet seems like a home run pitch. The products are small, non-perishable, low in weight and high in value, which makes third-party delivery to the home a comparatively simple, economical proposition.

Many prescription drugs and personal care items are purchased repeatedly, too, which plays to a major strength of the virtual store — the ability to save and access personal shopping lists. Throw in a relationship-building reminder feature, such as the excellent one at Drugstore.com, and repeat purchases should be assured.

Pure virtual drug store operators cite their lack of brick and mortar encumbrance as a competitive advantage. With no physical stores to staff and stock, lower transportation costs, and centralized inventory, they propose to reinvent drugstore merchandising online and carve away market share from the older, sluggish chains.

Within the scope of their vision, they're quite correct. But they are .COM entrepreneurs first and merchants second. In the rush for venture capital and IPO dollars, they tend to play down how most of the same factors make online selling a compelling opportunity for established chains too.

> The chain drug giants know how to squeeze out profits despite millions of dollars invested in infrastructure, human resources, and most significantly, inventory.

For a 4,100 store chain like CVS, the addition of a well-conceived virtual storefront like Soma.com is a bold leap into turnkey cyber-selling. The combination permits an order-here, pickup-there prescription service that pure virtual operators cannot offer. The online information flows can enhance in-store merchandising and promotion, and the stores themselves can promote use of the Web ordering option.

More decisive moves toward broadband drugstore merchandising are well underway.

Prescription renewals are already available on the Walgreens, Rite Aid and JC Penney (Eckerd Drug) sites. Recent press reports indicate that more product lines will be added in coming months. Drug Emporium has led the way with drugemporium.com, which sells over 16,000 items on-line, including prescription drugs, health and beauty aids, cosmetics and vitamins.

These chains have a huge leg up in brand identity compared with their purely virtual competitors. Every store is a billboard; the chains have pre-existing deals with many prescription plans; and most shoppers already have established pharmacy relationships.

The chain drug giants also have experience at operating at scale. They know how to squeeze out profits despite millions of dollars invested in infrastructure, human resources, and most significantly, inventory.

Pure virtual drugstores must establish their brands with consumers first, a marketing challenge which their own reports indicate soaks up the largest portion of their capital funding.

If they are fortunate enough to build market share, they will need to pour further sums into infrastructure, human resources, and the dreaded inventory. While they are at it, they had best watch their calendars, because they must find a way to earn a return on all that investment before their V.C. backers or IPO shareholders run out of patience.

No wonder the quick minds at Soma.com took the deal with CVS.

By spring of 1999 the notion that online retailers represented a new, competing and somehow superior class of retail trade was beginning to be displaced by a more realistic view. The editors at Executive Technology *magazine kindly allowed use of their soapbox in June of that year.*

WHEN BITS MEET MORTAR

DO VIRTUAL STORES CONSTITUTE a new competing class of retail trade? Or are they more a proving ground for a new skill set that all retailers will soon acquire? Aggressive moves into online selling by big brick-and-mortar operators suggest they see virtual storefronts as a means of leveraging, augmenting and protecting their consumer franchises. One might say they are using the Internet to broaden their retailing bandwidth.

The trend is well documented. In its Second Annual Internet Shopping Study, released earlier this year, Ernst & Young found that 65% of chain retailers surveyed were either already selling online by last December or expected to be in time for the 1999 Holiday rush.

Some operators who tiptoed defensively into the virtual realm last year are now beefing up their online presence. Two examples from recent headlines:

- Toys "R" Us, which was already selling online, announced plans in April to launch a stand-alone Internet unit in a bid to overtake upstart eToys and raise some .COM capital.

- Federated Department Stores, which already had made a splash with its Macys.com virtual store, completed its $1.7 billion acquisition of Fingerhut Cos. in March, gaining more than a dozen online specialty stores and a trove of expertise.

Venture capitalists and IPO day-traders may regard these chains as sluggish latecomers to the online world. But in going broad-band, chains pressure pure Vstores, who face the dual challenge of establishing their new brands with consumers and reaching profitability before their investors run out of patience.

The "first-mover advantage" so often trumpeted in IPO hype and Silicon Valley business plans may prove fleeting, as Internet-only retailers confront issues related to scale. As Amazon.com, eToys and CDNow are discovering, the bigger their turnover gets, the more dollars they must invest in infrastructure, human resources and inventory.

A melding of Vstore bits with chain's mortar seems like a virtual certainty.

Chain retailers understand and have lived with these financial realities. But, as the Web spin-offs by Toys "R" Us and Barnes & Noble signify, chains are also envious of the high valuations investors have placed on aspiring .COM retailers. They want a share of the speculative pie, and adding a flashy Vstore face is a good way to win favor on Wall Street.

While many chains possess the capital depth to develop Vstore proficiency on their own, the learning curve can be steep. A faster, smarter way to become a broadband merchant might be to follow Federated's lead and acquire the expertise fully formed and functioning.

Targets like Fingerhut won't come along every day. But many Vstore start-ups now making headlines evince capital "burn rates" which make them likely candidates to run dry of funds before achieving operational profitability. To survive, they will seek to leverage their creativity, technical expertise, and customer lists by forming alliances.

That's where alert chain retailers should have an opportunity to step in and shop for turnkey Vstore operations at favorable prices.

A melding of Vstore bits with chains' mortar? Seems like a virtual certainty.

A rare dip into the realm of communications theory, a.k.a. Media Ecology. The following Tirade appeared in VStoreNews *in February, 1999.*

EMBRACE COMPLEXITY, STUPID!

VSN WORLD HEADQUARTERS, WESTPORT, CT — Cybernetics is a term coined by mathematician Norbert Wiener for the study of control processes in electronic, mechanical and biological systems.

Wiener wrote brilliantly of this subject in his books *Cybernetics* (1948) and *The Human Use of Human Beings* (1950), and thereby created the underlying disciplines that led others to create digital computing and communications technologies. You might say that cybernetics begot cybershopping.

Cybernetic theory teaches us many things about what makes communications effective. I find particularly useful those principles which relate to improving the odds that a message is received and correctly understood. They apply equally well in device-to-device communications and in human-to-human communications. I would argue that they are central to retail success, virtual or terrestrial.

How do you get your message through better? Well for one, you can *turn up the power*. Up the signal strength. Shout. You can also *reduce the noise*. Filter out static. Take your conversation partner into a quiet room.

You can *repeat the message*. Hit the "re-send" key. Build redundant channels. State your ideas over and over until you are blue in the face.

You can provide a *mechanism for feedback*. This is the key difference between interactive, two-way media and passive, broadcast media. Listen to what you partner (or customer) says in response to your words or actions. Look them in the eye for a glimmer of understanding.

You can *add more bandwidth*. A bigger information pipe allows a more data to be sent. The richer the message, the better it may be understood. A telephone call is easier for most people to comprehend than a telegraph. If you gesture expressively while you talk, your partner is more likely to understand the meaning behind your words.

All of these techniques add complexity to the message or the messaging process in order to improve communications. A worthwhile tradeoff, I'd say. It's why we put talk-back links on our Web sites. It's why many of us dream of a wide-band Internet that will carry rich interactive shopping experiences into people's homes.

The oft-cited K.I.S.S. principle: "Keep It Simple, Stupid" comes off as too simple and too stupid in the context of the Vstore reality.

It's also why it makes sense that many existing retail chains are adding cyber-storefronts — they provide another way to interact with consumers on their terms: More bandwidth means an additional channel of communications with shoppers. More volume, less noise means a more intense, exclusive shopping experience for those consumers who choose to use this channel. More mechanism for feedback — well the interactivity of the Internet is ideal for this.

Interestingly, the term "cyber," as in cyberspace, cybersex and cybershop, is derived from a shortening of Wiener's terminology. He in turn derived it from the Greek *kybernetes*, which means "steersman" or controller. So cyber indirectly refers to control.

Ironic, eh? To this observer, the World Wide Web seems anything *but* controlled. It's a writhing, seething communications organism, with few rules or limitations. No wonder bricks-and-mortar retailers were initially skittish about online selling. It seemed too complex. Too uncontrolled.

That's changing fast. As Ernst & Young reported last month in *its Second Annual Internet Shopping Study*, 39% of surveyed retailers began offering online shopping during 1998. Another 37% have plans to do so — two thirds of them during 1999.

These findings indicate that major retailers now understand how imperative it is that they embrace the complexity that goes along with operating a virtual storefront. They recognize how adding an online presence broadens the bandwidth of their shopper interaction. They accept the systems, logistical and supplier relations challenges that this implies. They are determined to compete effectively with the new breed of pure online retailers, by leveraging their brand equity, capital depth, and merchandising know-how to press their advantage.

As for the oft-cited K.I.S.S. principle: "Keep It Simple, Stupid" comes off as too simple and too stupid in the context of the Vstore reality.

Wiener's work suggests that when it comes to effective communications and control, simplicity is not the answer. Reflexive opposition of complexity may in fact be the more perilous course.

My Advice?

Kiss off the K.I.S.S. principle. Bandwidth has value. Purposeful complexity can pay off.

By the middle of 1998 the mainstream media had discovered online retailing. By the pre-holiday period, the coverage grew into a near-frenzy of speculation and pseudo-analysis. I felt a need to propagate a more reasoned point of view. This column appeared in RT *magazine in December 1998, just as the holiday surge peaked.*

Virtual Retailing Must Deliver Real Value

Vstores that learn how to efficiently accept, consolidate and deliver orders made up of multiple SKUs have an opportunity to add value in the online world

THE NEWS FLOW ABOUT THE virtual store business really heated up this summer. Suddenly mainstream publications like *Time*, the *Wall Street Journal* and *New York Times* began carrying major features declaring that Internet shopping is the Next Great Thing.

"Kiss Your Mall Goodbye," read the cover line on the July 20 issue of *Time*, "Online shopping is faster cheaper and better."

The *Journal* went so far as to identify a "Cyber-squeeze" on profit margins for Web retailers in a front page article which appeared the same week.

The Times called Internet shopping "a mixed bag" and declared that "The Virtual Mall is still under construction."

Business pages across the country carried stories about strategic moves of online retailers, as well as Vstore entries by mainstream retailers such as Macy's, Toys "R" Us and Barnes & Noble.

Suddenly every high-traffic Internet site wanted to become a "portal," and the major ones like Yahoo! and America Online are making lucrative promotional deals with online retailers such as Amazon.com and CDNow.

Internet research company MediaMetrix reported that some 20 million American cybernauts visited Vstores from their home computers in 1997. They bought some $2.6 billion worth of goods online, according to Jupiter Communications, New York, or $2.4 billion worth, according to Forrester Research. Projections for the future are so divergent as to be unreliable. Web retail volume could reach $35 billion by 2002, or it could be $100 billion from the U.S. alone, or it could be $300 billion worldwide. Or make up your own number and paste it into your IPO documents.

> Vstores that learn how to efficiently accept, consolidate and deliver orders made up of multiple SKUs have an opportunity to add value to the online go-to-market system.

The volume on this story may be turned up high, but to supermarket and mass retailers, I suspect it's mostly noise. Let's be realistic about this: Forrester estimates current food and beverage sales on the web amount to just $168 million per year — roughly the volume of four or five successful supermarkets.

Furthermore, mainstream analyses of online retailing tend to emphasize high-margin product categories like books, CDs and computers over those with high volume and rapid turnover. All these products are ordered and shipped individually direct to the consumer using a third-party delivery service like UPS or Fedex.

On the other hand, as the companies involved in Andersen Consulting's well known "Consumer Direct" project learned for their considerable fees, this is not a practical model for selling boxes of Tide or bottles of Coke. The issue here is common to any product with a modest price point and a low gross margin: The cost of fulfillment would exceed the profit on the sale.

Think about it. An average household typically purchases its groceries from among 150 items. Should the UPS man deliver a separate, carefully packed box for each jar of mustard, can of beans, sack of frozen French fries? The cost of the packing materials alone would obviate any profits.

And despite convincing arguments about disintermediation (geek-speak for "cutting out the middle man") it will never be practical to deliver fast-turn, low margin products direct from the manufacturer.

Vstores that learn how to efficiently accept, consolidate and deliver orders made up of multiple SKUs have an opportunity to add value to the online go-to-market system, just as the best chain retailers do in the physical world.

The online consumer gets a lower price, the Vstore and manufacturer earn better profits, and competing "brick and mortar" retailers must adapt to a world of even sharper prices while conceding a few percent of sales to the next class of trade.

This list first appeared on the VStoreNews.com Web site in the spring of 1998. It became the basis for a series of talks I delivered that year. Thirteen — that perilous number — was a deliberate choice. I am pleased to observe that the validity of these observations have held up decently with the passage of time.

THIRTEEN THINGS EVERY RETAILER AND BRAND MARKETER NEEDS TO KNOW ABOUT VSTORES

1) EVERY SIGNIFICANT NEW CHANNEL of retail trade introduced over the past 200 years has shared a common type of innovation: Through the use of mass economies, new technologies or both, each succeeded in providing products to consumers for a better overall value than the channels they displaced. In other words, they sold goods under a lower gross margin structure but earned greater profits due to greater turnover and larger volume.

2) CONTRARY TO MOST published analyses to date, the biggest Vstore opportunities lie not with the highest-priced or highest-margin products, but with the most frequently-purchased products, i.e. grocery and non-food consumables.

3) ONLY A FEW PERCENT OF CONSUMER SPENDING has to shift from "brick & mortar" stores to virtual shopping for a major economic displacement to ensue.

4) ONLY A MINORITY OF CONSUMERS has to change their shopping habits for a few percent of the market to shift.

5) THOSE CONSUMERS NEED ONLY CHANGE PART of their shopping behavior to account for the critical mass needed — Doing half one's shopping on line may be enough.

6) IT'S ALREADY EASIER and more pleasant to buy many things on-line than at the store — and virtual store technology and esthetics are still in their infancy.

7) CONVENIENCE IS ALREADY a more valuable currency than money for many consumers, but Virtual Stores can deliver convenience without sacrificing competitive pricing.

8) SECURITY CONCERNS about on-line credit card purchases are purely psychological — and they are prone to exaggeration by conventional businesses that have no other strategy to compete with Vstores.

9) SELLING IT ONLINE IS THE EASY PART. Fulfilling the order efficiently is the real challenge — and a great opportunity for software and logistics companies.

10) THE VSTORE OPERATOR(S) who perfect methods of delivering frequently-purchased goods (i.e. groceries) to consumers, will thereby create a new delivery system which will displace the commercial package delivery services as the preferred mode of delivering other products sold on line.

11) THE RISE OF VIRTUAL STORES will have a serious detrimental impact on the commercial real estate markets during the next 5 years, by skimming away a portion of sales from marginally-performing "brick and mortar" stores which will be forced to close.

12) CONSUMER PRODUCT MANUFACTURERS will have no choice but to adjust their go-to-market systems, sales contracts, deal terms, promotional strategies, packaging, pricing, and sales organizations to contend with these emerging realities.

13) EVERY COMPANY whose business is derived by serving the needs listed in #12 will have to adjust as well, and that includes advertising and promotion agencies, sales agencies, marketing consultants, logistics companies, printers, contract manufacturers, in-store merchandising firms, packaging manufacturers, store design companies, investors, and real estate developers.

Online shopping had its awareness breakthrough in the fall of 1998, as suddenly the mainstream media discovered the Internet's potential to revolutionize a major category of human interaction. This Tirade appeared in the November VStoreNews.

YES, DULLES, VIRGINIA. THERE IS A SANITY CLAUSE

VSN WORLD HEADQUARTERS, WESTPORT, CT — Well here I go again, torturing the English language in a headline until our readers beg for mercy. Who else would dare sully one of American journalism's most cherished sentimental moments by melding an underhanded jab at America Online with the over-the-top zanyness of Groucho Marx?

Not to pick unfairly on AOL. It's just that it is based in Virginia, which makes the headline work. Besides, it connects more consumers to the Web than any other provider. It's the biggest and richest aggregator in cyberland, so why not use it rhetorically as a symbolic "every-portal"?

AOL (like Yahoo!, Excite, and the rest of the audience aggregators out there, great and small) is lurching headlong into what history may someday judge to be the actual birth tremors of the virtual store revolution. There's no denying that Vstores have been incubating in the World Wide Womb for a number of years now, but this year, this Holiday Season, they have emerged kicking and yelling to claim their birthright.

This will be remembered as The $3 Billion Season. A heady 6 million households will launch their credit card numbers across the 'Net. The prospect of paying for and delivering all those virtual purchases has executives at Visa, MasterCard, UPS and FedEx rubbing their hands and hiring temps.

If you monitor the press releases, surf a bit, or read your spam, you can't help but notice. Special new holiday shopping pages are springing up like mushrooms. It seems like every Web site with more than a thousand visitors a week is trying to get into the act — usually not as sellers of goods themselves, but as "distribution points" for other existing Vstore operators.

Most conspicuous in this are the above-mentioned "portals" and the creators of virtual "communities" like Tripod (www.tripod.com), The Globe (www.theglobe.com), and Geocities (www.geocities.com). Each of these services has gathered links to a hundred or so well-known and less well-known Vstores into its own on-line shopping center, or mall.

Hand onto your strategies, folks. Next month's holiday sales reports may send everybody back to the drawing boards.

A comparison with the world of bricks and mortar is apt here: Many of the same retail nameplates repeat from e-mall to e-mall — logos for well-known virtual store brands like Amazon.com, Barnes & Noble, Egghead.com, CDNow, OfficeDepot.com, and eToys all turn up repeatedly. In the typical arrangement, instead of rent, mall operators collect "referral fees" — essentially commissions on sales made to shoppers who link in from the mall-owner's site. Just like in the brick and mortar world, the mall operator's responsibility is to generate traffic, while the stores kick a cut of sales back to the landlord.

This arrangement has proven a boon to Internet companies, who finally can show a source of tangible revenues to their venture capitalists and public investors. In unprecedented fashion, virtual store sales (what the great unwashed masses call "e-commerce") are propping up many 'Net companies' preposterous shareholder values. And just in the nick of time, because online advertising sales (you remember them — last year's rationale for preposterous shareholder values?) are not materializing as forecast in many Silicon Valley business plans.

The nub of it is: The big aggregators are not succeeding particularly well at selling advertising to *real* consumer brands — you know, like Tide, Coca Cola and Nabisco. Yes there has been a good bit of banner advertising from the likes of Ford and ATT, but the dollar values are really minor. In recent weekly reports from Net Ratings (www.netratings.com) the top ten banner ads have consistently been placed by other Internet brands — mainly Vstores and software companies.

The aggregators' business plans promise shareholders and VC backers that ad revenues will spiral upwards, but real world consumer brand marketers are coming to this medium a bit tentatively, unimpressed as they are with the value of hits and clicks. As a result of poor demand and growing inventories, the cost per click is spiraling … *downwards.*

It's as if the Big Brands are thinking, "Who needs the aggregation?"

Okay, okay, we're torturing The Language again. But no doubt, many major consumer brands can and do drive bigger audiences to their web sites by tagging their URL's to a few of their own magazine and television ads.

In unprecedented fashion, virtual store sales are propping up many 'Net companies' preposterous shareholder values.

So why the swipe at AOL in the headline? Call it VSN Holiday Spirit. Our friends in Dulles, VA are making real money off their so-called distribution deals with leading Vstore operators. For the moment at least, they and the other portals seem to have cracked the ever-changing code.

So here's the Sanity Clause: Right now it looks like collecting commissions from online sales is the best — maybe the only way — to make money on the Internet. Big advertising revenues remain somewhere over the rainbow — and there they will stay, as long as marketing on the World Wide Web remains as inward-looking and self-referential as it is today.

My Advice?

Hang onto your strategies, folks.

Next month's holiday sales reports may send everybody back to the drawing boards.

Autumn of 1998 saw a near frenzy of media coverage of the online retail phenomenon, and a whole new industry was born with the mission of measuring it. It reached a crescendo as the holiday sales season approached, sparking this commentary in the November VStoreNews.

HTTP, HOLIDAY HYPE AND HERALDRY

WORLD WIDE WEB — How does that song go again? *"They know when you've been surfing. They know when you're in chat. They know what you've been buying, so for goodness sakes be discreet about that!"...*

If the volume and ubiquity of Holiday Hype is any indication, a host of major cyber-players and cyber-seers have determined that this is the pivotal season for holiday shopping online. And the trends — well they had better not cry about those (*I'm telling you why*):

First, the forecasts. Allowing for the general lack of methodological rigor evinced by most of the research houses that are currently tracking web commerce, most are generally on the same page with their holiday sales projections, once you untangle their definitions.

New York-based Cyber Dialogue (www.cyberdialogue.com) said in a November report that some 12 billion Americans will "rely on the Internet" for holiday shopping, "impacting" some $5 billion in total spending. *VStoreNews* applauds the careful wording of this release, since it addresses the cumulative impact of the Internet on total purchasing, not just actual online sales.

"Contrary to conventional wisdom, many retail stores will actually benefit from the Internet, during this holiday shopping season," Cyber Dialogue reported. It went on to assert that 6.7 million adults would purchase holiday items online this year. It also forecast that 9.0 million shoppers would purchase products in stores after first gathering information online.

Just a few days earlier, Forrester Research, Inc. (www.forrester.com) had predicted that online retail sales for the fourth quarter of 1998 would reach $3.5 billion, making 1998 "a pivotal year in the evolution of e-commerce." Here the figure appears to blend Holiday gift sales with routine online sales. An aggressive number, but we think it is fairly realistic.

As usual in this market sector, reliable numbers are hard to come by, what with varying methodologies and definitions of terms. Still, logarithmic growth seems inevitable, considering that the major portals have been adding huge numbers of links to their shopping areas. Yahoo! for example, said it had attracted more than 3,000 merchants to its Yahoo Shopping Area between Nov. 15 and Dec. 18. Like many major Internet players, it has been promoting its services online, on TV and in print.

It seems that this surge in off-line advertising by Vstores and portals is perhaps the major story of the season.

The *New York Times* reported on the front page of its Nov. 25 business section that America Online had designs on fostering online shopping growth by offering Vstore hosting services to new and existing retailers. Explained AOL President Bob Pittman in a pre-Thanksgiving news conference, "We see a major business in offering them an end-to-end solution."

Offline advertising and promotions by established and emergent Vstore operators have reached a fever pitch in December. Especially frequent are radio spots for TV, print and radio spots for Priceline.com, radio ads for CDNow (www.cdnow.com), newspaper ads by Value America (www.valueamerica.com), and our favorite television spots by software seller Outpost.com.

We especially enjoy the latter example, for its unabashed political incorrectness. The most memorable spot involves the firing of gerbils from a cannon aimed at an opening in an Outpost.com billboard. It takes about five misses before the shooter succeeds in propelling a hapless rodent through the center of the letter O. (The remaining gerbils appear to survive the indignity and scurry away.)

Beyond the very promising Vstore traffic reports and sales projections we have seen so far, it seems that this surge in off-line advertising by Vstores and portals is perhaps the major story of the season. Just when it seemed as if the Internet advertising community was smugly engrossed in its "navel-gazing" ways (a characterization which must be duly credited to Chan Suh, chairman of New York based interactive ad shop, Agency.com), a few of the smartest cyber-marketers have lifted their heads and brought their branding propositions out to the people.

They understand that there is no e-branding. There is only branding. And branding — whether on or off the Internet — is certainly of crucial importance. The enormous unaided awareness among all consumers of brands like Priceline and Amazon.com is not primarily due to these companies' online marketing activities, but rather to their assertive (and expensive) offline public relations and advertising campaigns.

Next month we'll take a look at the holiday sales reports and try to analyze the multiple lines of force that are driving this market sector headlong into unexplored territory.

The rise of Internet advertising was closely tied to the rise of the virtual store for several reasons. Each reflected a rather desperate effort by pioneering Internet audience aggregators to find a way to earn some revenues from the new medium. In the November 1998 VStoreNews, *I offered some commentary.*

BEYOND PORTALS AND COMMUNITIES — VSTORES

VSN WORLD HEADQUARTERS, WESTPORT, CT — The plot is really thickening in the new "marketspace" of the Internet. The next Really Big Thing is turning out to be virtual store retailing. But not only for the reasons you already suspect.

True, virtual store sales are surging. But so far, the profits are slim to non-existent, and the business impact is lagging well behind the hype.

Some 48 million American cybernauts visited Vstores from their home computers in 1997. That's roughly one-fifth of the country. They'll buy some $4.8 billion worth of goods online in all of 1998, according to a recent study from Nielsen Media Research.

And the projections for the fourth quarter of this year are nothing short of stellar, with shoppers expected to spend some $2.3 billion online during the 1998 holiday season, according to research released last week by Jupiter Communications, New York.

A separate study from eMarketer, New York predicts that up to 29% of the total year's online sales will come in the November-December period, or perhaps 1% percent of the $173 billion take forecast for the holiday period by Deloitte & Touche in its survey for the National Retail Federation.

Now, $4.8 billion remains a mere rounding error in the total consumer goods marketplace of roughly $1.5 trillion (U.S. Dept. of Commerce). What is promising about these numbers is that an increasing fraction of the American buying public may now be reached in the virtual store, where the message may be delivered at the moment of decision.

For brand marketers and web marketers this is an opportunity of the first order. Its magnitude will make the successes of the so-called "portal" sites like Yahoo!, AOL and Excite! and "community" sites like Geocities and Tripod seem like mere steps in the continuum.

These Internet audience "aggregators" are creating shareholder value based on their present or projected abilities to deliver consumers to advertisers. But no form of media today does a better job of putting consumers in front of promotional messages than retail stores.

Brand marketers know this intuitively — that's why they spend 50% of their promotional dollars on retail trade promotion activities, a fact just reconfirmed in Cox Direct's *20th Annual Survey of Promotional Practices*. Virtual stores can be just as effective in this regard as brick and mortar stores.

Not that traditional advertising won't have an impact online. Last summer's FAST Summit, the gathering on the future of Internet advertising hosted by Procter & Gamble, opened many eyes to the potential of brand equity advertising on the Internet.

To some degree, traditional media models apply. With some 79 million current Internet users in the U.S. and Canada according to Nielsen Media Research, purveyors of brands can certainly access mass audiences on line.

There are also unprecedented factors: mass-customization — the ability to speak to many consumers on a one-to-one basis; and interactivity — the ability to allow consumers to select which message elements they choose to view and respond to.

At a series of events since then, most recently the @d:tech conference in New York, many of the same "advertising stakeholders" have viewed the latest in Internet advertising technology. New developments in so-called "rich media," a set of tools for packing more visual and interactive punch into the banners and pop-up windows that decorate the portals and communities of the World Wide Web.

Where the objective is to deliver a memorable brand message to a passively viewing consumer, the 'Net can hardly compete with good ol' TV. But for the web surfer, who sits forward in her chair controlling the flow of content, carefully delivered rich media ads certainly have potential to advance marketers' brand equity objectives.

What many advertising stakeholders overlook, however, is that the Internet is much more than a new medium of communications. It is also simultaneously a medium of transactions. That means its potential use for trade promotion messaging could dwarf its use for straight, brand equity advertising.

For the first time in the history of human communications (giving homage to Marshall McLuhan), The Medium is the Market.

> Web marketing strategists had best consider the models that will enable trade marketing to translate seamlessly into the Vstore environment.

As Vstores attract larger numbers of high-value consumers to their online emporiums, brand marketers will recognize that their messages must reach consumers at the virtual point of sale. Smart online retailers — notably those with deep brick and mortar experience like @lbertsons.com and Wal-Mart.com, will sense this opportunity and arrive in buying meetings with rate cards in hand.

What's a virtual endcap worth? What about a virtual coupon delivered at the virtual shelf? What about targeted email delivered to virtual shopper club members? What's the payment model for these instruments?

Trade marketing professionals had better prepare to answer these questions if they are to translate their brand strategies into effective trade strategies for the Vstore channel. Web marketing strategists had best consider the models that will enable trade marketing to translate seamlessly into the Vstore environment.

My Advice?

Recognize the Vstore for all that it is — both market and medium.

Vstore activity in the drug store and personal care segment proved a litmus test for online retailing overall. This commentary ran in the Nov. 1998 issue of VStoreNews.

SHAMPOO'S SWELL, BUT CAN YOU EMAIL AN EGG CREAM?

MUCH-HYPED VIRTUAL RETAILER Drugstore.com may have its hands full defending itself against a highly-publicized legal challenge from Wal-Mart Stores, which has accused the start-up of illegally recruiting retail information systems experts from its Bentonville, AR headquarters. No matter that Wal-Mart has levied the same debatable charge against Amazon.com, it's tough being made an example of.

Perhaps due to its high profile president and CEO — Peter Neupert, a former top Microsoft exec — and its high profile VC backers — Kleiner Perkins Caufield & Byer — Drugstore.com may be the most hotly anticipated of a new crew of drug and HBC retailers now reaching the virtual marketspace.

In fact, the Silicon Valley startup is coming a bit late to the race, having been beaten out of the blocks by several significant national competitors, including Drug Emporium the Columbus, OH based deep-discount drug chain, and HomePharmacy.com, based in Vienna, VA.

Now Neupert & Co. must add another Vstore to its radar screen: Mybasics.com, a New York-based startup company, which obtained its domain name in August and hung out its virtual shingle in mid-October.

The Mybasics site offers some 7,000 name brand health and beauty items at discounts it says are up to 25% below typical retail prices — meaning it is competitive with chain drug stores, but aiming to be the every-day low price leader. It is also notable for its against-the-grain-of-the-Web orientation toward female shoppers, who do most of the HBC shopping in the "real" world.

So far this Vstore carries only OTC remedies and personal care items, but there are hints that it could be filling prescriptions in short order. For one, Mybasics.com is supplied by AmeriSource, Malvern, PA, the nation's fourth largest drug and HBC wholesaler.

AmeriSource is already an adept in the prescription drug business and operates some 23 distribution centers around the country. Through its Rita Ann division, it is also a significant supplier of cosmetics to the mass market. (In case you had been following the story: Yes, this is the same AmeriSource whose planned merger with #1 wholesaler McKesson was scuttled earlier this year by the Federal Government over antitrust concerns.)

Drugstore products are also consumables, like groceries, which makes them a natural for planned replenishment.

Background information on company principal and Chairman Lehmann Li has been hard to come by, but company spokeswoman Ashley Hyland did consent to a brief interview at the company's Manhattan offices one week after the site debuted. She confirmed that Mybasics.com is privately funded and described some well-considered initial marketing efforts for the brand.

For starters, the company cut a deal with iVillage.com, for a placement on that women's community site's revamped Shopping Channel page, which debuted Nov. 2. Not bad, considering that this places Mybasics.com alongside such "established" Vstore brands as 1-800-Flowers, Amazon.com, Net Grocer and Music Boulevard.

Hyland said the company plans another promotional wave using BonusMail, the "dialog" marketing vehicle from Intellipost, San Francisco, which now claims 750,000 consumers enrolled in its database. Enrollees in this program agree to accept targeted email in exchange for awards credits similar to airline miles.

What's nice about virtual HBA retailing, she noted, is the low weight-to-price ratio and non-perishability of the merchandise, which makes it easy for the company to offer free UPS shipping on orders above $50 (initial orders are shipped free as well). Yet these products are also consumables, like groceries, which makes them a natural for planned replenishment.

That's a core service offering at Mybasics. Called, "basics-backup," the plan allows consumers to set up a regular monthly order list. Users may specify whether each item on the list should be re-supplied on a monthly, bimonthly or every-three-month basis. Mybasics sends plan members a monthly email reminder, a few days prior to shipment, which allows the customer to make any needed modifications.

"There is high brand loyalty in this category," Hyland explained. "There is less decision making at the shelf if the products are priced right. It's a repeat purchase, not a new decision each time."

VStoreNews *made its official debut as a paid-subscription e-periodical in July 1998. Its release coincided with the first big demonstration of interest in the e-retailing phenomenon by the general business media. I took pains to demonstrate a deeper familiarity with the retail marketplace in this Tirade.*

MARGIN TO HELL (FOR A HEAVENLY CAUSE)

VSN WORLD HEADQUARTERS, WESTPORT, CT — The impossible dream is coming true. Just when you thought retail margin structures couldn't be shaved any lower, here come the heroic Vstores. They have no bricks, no mortar, sometimes even no inventory to weigh them down, and they're selling the same old products for even less than the chains.

Consumers get lower prices. Conventional retailers gulp air and try to cinch their suppliers' belts down a notch. Manufacturers re-engineer their sales forces (again). And the rest of the players in the go-to-market system keep jockeying for position.

I'm telling you, it's like club stores déjà vu all over again. How long can these guys keep selling stuff for less than it costs? Remember 20 years ago when Sol Price, Jim Sinegal and the boys started selling those huge cereal boxes and cases of copier paper at unit prices that made the supermarkets and office supply houses pull their hair out? I knew a "famous brand" sunglass manufacturer who actually took to buying his merchandise back from the shelves at club store retail, just to keep his small optician customers from screaming bloody murder and boycotting his line (but that's another story).

It took a few years, but they spawned widespread industry reaction. Club packs started appearing on supermarket shelves (usually at loss-leader price points). EDLP champion Wal-Mart decided it had to have a leading position in the club business itself. Industry-wide initiatives were initiated, with impressive-sounding names written by committees, like "Efficient Consumer Response." Huge consulting windfalls were raked in by pundits clever enough to interpret the auguries and invent infernally complex solutions. Conferences were organized. New trade publications were launched.

Just like in any war. Some people get killed. Some get rich.

If you are reading this inaugural edition of *VStoreNews* — this newsletter being the first trade publication anywhere solely devoted to untangling the implications of the virtual store revolution — then I am betting that you're planning on being one of the rich ones this time around.

You've been following the impressive sales increases reported by online bookseller, Amazon.com. You've heard the radio ads from CDNow and read the articles about Macys.com. You've clicked on the Yahoo! and Excite shopping channels and explored the hundreds of links there from VStores offering everything from prime steaks to plastic flamingoes. You've bought shares of Dell Computer Corporation and watched them soar.

With some of the stock market's highest price-to-earnings ratios emanating from Internet commerce (witness Amazon and Yahoo!'s breathtaking multiples), now even the mainstream media are discovering Virtual Store Retailing. Why in the past week alone we saw front-page articles in *Time*, the *Wall Street Journal*, and the *New York Times* business section.

"Kiss Your Mall Goodbye," declared the *Time* cover line, "Online shopping is faster, cheaper and better." (That rumble you hear is the sound of thousands of brick and mortar retailers' hearts pounding in unison.)

The *Times* insisted, "Virtual Stores Give the Big Retailers A Foothold Against On-Line Upstarts," as it documented the feverish competition now brewing in the toy category. Now even Toys "R" Us, which was slow getting out of the box, has got Vstore functionality on its Web site. Christmas shopping will never be the same (thank goodness).

But the *Journal* writer George Anders really nailed the situation with his "Cybersqueeze" analogy: "The very things that attract us to the Internet — speed, convenience, and unlimited breadth — make it treacherous for profit-hungry merchants. With just a few keystrokes, consumers can play business rivals against each other. That ability is turning the Net into a relentlessly efficient market in which vendors will be hard-pressed to win, and defend, any lasting competitive advantage."

Wow. He's almost got the whole picture there. Just one more logical step and he would have distilled the huge impact Internet retailing is about to have on all retailing. Gross margins as we know them are all in jeopardy. Not just for VStores, but for every competing retailer, regardless of format.

Gross margins as we know them are all in jeopardy. Not just for VStores, but for every competing retailer, regardless of format.

Like the club stores before them, virtual stores represent the trigger for a whole new margin structure for consumer products retailing. Like club stores were two decades ago, VStores are the Next Channel. They will bleed away a fraction of the conventional retailers business in the next couple of years — maybe 3% maybe 5% — and that $70 billion will be enough to change everything.

Find that analysis to be a stretch? Well consider its three key corollaries:

1) *The biggest Vstore opportunities lie not with the highest-priced or highest-margin products, but with the most frequently-purchased products.* Most households will spend more on consumable products like groceries year in and year out than they will in any other consumer category. Buying

groceries could be the "killer app" that will bring online shopping to the masses.

2) *Only a few percent of consumer spending has to shift from "brick and mortar" stores to virtual shopping for a major economic displacement to ensue.* That's because so many stores are surviving on the brink already that to sustain a loss of a small percentage of their best customers could put them out of business.

3) *Product marketers will have to adjust their go-to-market systems, pricing, sales contracts, deal terms, promotional strategies, sales organizations and packaging, to contend with these emerging realities.* When the underlying economics change, the rules have to change too.

Now, there are a lot of folks out there wondering if any retailers are going to get rich in a world populated by VStores. After all, Amazon.com isn't showing any profits. Neither is Peapod. Is making money selling consumer products on the Internet an impossible dream? Will "relentlessly efficient" consumer pricing simply drive all profitability out of the consumer value chain?

I'm prepared to offer a bold prediction, based on history and speculation: Vstores will rise, causing gross margins to drop. New efficiencies will be developed that will radically redefine the value chain for consumer goods. Some retail companies will be casualties of war. But some others will find the right formula of marketing, sales, transaction and fulfillment to make it work. They and their investors will get rich, and consumers will get even better prices and services.

My Advice?

Expect everything to change, and faster than you would believe.

VStoreNews *made its pre-publication debut In May of 1998 in the form of a four-page issue, which was distributed mostly by hand at trade shows. This brief essay set the tone for what would follow and defined the agenda that the publication would pursue for the next four years.*

ARE YOU READY FOR THE NEXT CHANNEL?

BOSTON-BASED Forrester Research says it was $450 million in 1997 and will be $4.3 billion in 1998. The organizers of eBusinessWorld estimate $1.35 billion last year among consumers, more than $7 billion in business-to-business. Virtual booksellers alone raked in $290 million last year.

What is the reality of online consumer shopping? The disparities in published data render them near useless. Trouble is, they are being developed not by retailing or marketing experts, but by computer industry analysts.

Even worse, the ill-considered terminology of "Consumer Direct" has poisoned the thinking of many consumer goods brand marketers who were seduced by the brilliant reasoning of "disintermediation" — the notion put forth by MIT Media Lab professor and *Wired* magazine columnist Nicholas Negroponte that the Internet would permit manufacturers to market and sell their products directly to the consumer without an intermediary.

Translation: "How do we do it? By cutting out the middle man!"

If you are a mass market retailer, haven't you heard this before? It may be elegant computer/communications theory, but it is not a very insightful analysis of the retailing industry.

The fact is, Consumer Direct and disintermediation neglect a factor in human culture which has persisted for millennia: Middle men — retailers, wholesalers, distributors — exist for good reason. They provide valuable services — order consolidation, warehousing, billing and transportation — that add value to the distribution chain and can reduce the cost of goods to the end consumer.

The fact is that even in an on-line world, virtual stores will do the same. Vgrocers like Streamline, NetGrocer, Homeruns, and others like them will succeed to the extent that they eliminate handling and distribution costs and efficiently bring goods to the consumer at competitive prices.

What we like to call "terrestrial" retailers face a new competitive challenge which already rivals the early days of the membership club business in 1979. Within 24 months, it could rival the club business today, at more than $100 billion. The forces are converging. The ascendancy of the next channel is inevitable.

My advice?

Be an antidisintermediationist.

When VStoreNews *was announced in Spring 1998 and it had the good fortune to attract some curiosity among some influential people. Among those was the leadership of the Association of Sales & Marketing Companies, which kindly invited me to address their executive conference that July. This feature article, a kind of mini-manifesto, appeared simultaneously in the association's magazine,* Sales & Marketing Quarterly, *that Summer.*

WHY VIRTUAL STORES MEAN REAL DOLLARS

Mainstream analyses of on-line shopping underplay the importance of grocery sales over the Internet. Trading partners should prepare now for a vastly different future market.

THE SKEPTICS WILL ARGUE convincingly that grocery shopping over the Internet hasn't exactly taken the world by storm. Despite some promising early results from virtual supermarkets like Chicago-based Peapod, Boston's Streamline and New York-headquartered Net Grocer, only a few hundred thousand households have ever experienced buying groceries on-line. Fewer buy food this way on any regular basis.

The demise last March of OnCart (formerly known as Shoppers Express), which had promised to be another major factor in the nascent Vgrocer business, adds credence to the argument that on-line food shopping is today but a minor factor for the industry. Peapod, the market leader with more than 103,000 consumers signed up at last report, reported a net loss of $4 million for the first quarter of 1998.

So the doubtful view seems realistic, even at a time when pundits from Andersen Consulting, Ernst & Young and Goldman Sachs address industry gatherings and publish reports declaring that "etailing" or "Consumer Direct" will be the Next Big Thing for the supermarket industry.

Furthermore, most analysts of the on-line shopping phenomenon — ranging from Forrester Research in Boston and Jupiter in New York, to the abovementioned consultants — place food and household consumables fairly far down on their lists of categories most likely to succeed over the Internet.

Books, recorded music and computer hardware and software are generally seen as the top opportunities, based on the early successes of Vstore operators like Amazon.com, CDNow, and Dell Computer Corporation. Grocery items, they argue, are comparatively low ticket and low margin — not the best prospects for home delivery. As we will explore below, the pundits miss a major point in their analyses

Healthy skepticism on this subject is a good thing, but it shouldn't stand in the way of a proactive business outlook. Despite a modest start, there is a sea change building in the Virtual Store world that could require existing supermarket retailers and their suppliers to completely re-engineer their go-to-market systems within the next five years.

Sales and marketing companies, which have turned their skill at adapting to changing market conditions into a near art form, will see their businesses affected as well. Virtual retailing is the next new class of retail trade. Someone is going to have to supply this channel with merchandise — and a lot of it.

Realistic Assumptions

It would be foolish to maintain that on-line food shopping will become a universal consumer practice in this country. But we can realistically argue that a large enough minority of consumers will change their shopping habits that the economics of the grocery business could be radically redefined.

Here's an analysis which reveals this potential: If only 10% of consumers choose to purchase *half* their grocery needs on line within three years, that would pull 5%, or $23 billion, in retail sales from the brick-and-mortar grocery universe. (This assumes total supermarket and other food store sales of $460 billion annually, based on U.S. Dept. of Commerce figures.)

This is a conservative estimate, since the profile of active Internet shoppers tends toward upscale, time-pressed, dual-income families — not coincidentally the same profile as most supermarkets' heaviest-buying customers. Applying a variant of the time-honored 80/20 rule to the above analysis makes plausible a doubling of that estimate to $46 billion.

Early results cited by Net Grocer and Peapod tend to support this behavior profile, at least among leading edge Vstore shoppers. Executives from both virtual supermarket operators have reported average tickets well above the norms for "terrestrial" stores.

It is already clear in Chicago and Boston, two markets where Peapod and Streamline have made the greatest inroads, that companies offering internet-based home delivery of groceries can skim away a portion of the brick-and-mortar stores' best customers.

This raises thought-provoking questions for existing supermarket operators: What is the impact upon existing businesses when the Vgrocers reach critical mass in a particular market? How many currently operating supermarkets could sustain the loss of 5% to 10% of their volume and still remain viable? In an era of over-stored markets, what percentage of supermarkets already operates on the brink? What would it take to push them over?

Manufacturers and their sales representatives face their own delicate issues with this development. The new Vstore channel will be hungry for merchandise. A handful of significant new accounts will emerge ready to buy quantity. Some of them will sell the same brands at sharper prices due to some of the inherent economies of on-line selling. Others will offer parity pricing with the market leaders combined with enhanced services. Existing conventional retailers, who are ceding share to these new upstarts, can hardly look kindly at a supplier who sells to them.

This potential conflict is already simmering beneath the surface. When Tim Dorgan, executive vice president of Peapod, the nation's largest on-line grocer with more than 100,000 consumer members, addressed an educational session at the 1998 Food Marketing Institute Convention in Chicago, this May, an audience member made the issue quite clear.

How can Peapod purport to be advancing the interests of its local supermarket operator partners, said the questioner, while at the same time it says it is developing dedicated fulfillment centers in its major markets? Dorgan, quite rightly and politely, expressed complete support for Peapod's retail partners, but judging by the murmurs in the audience, his reply seemed not to satisfy. Neither were other panel members, from Andersen, Information Resources Inc., Streamline, Ahold and Ralston Purina, quick to jump to his defense.

Other Evolutionary Challenges

To be fair, Peapod's evolutionary challenges must be viewed as matters of due course. After all, this is not the first time in our generation that a new class of retail trade has emerged to threaten the status quo. Nearly twenty years ago, food brokers and manufacturer sales reps in Southern California faced a similar painful dilemma.

A crafty old merchant named Sol Price had opened a new type of retail store in San Diego that threatened to undermine the status quo. A bare-bones warehouse building with a limited assortment of large-sized packages, steel rack shelving, full pallet displays and bare concrete floors, the Price Club sold goods at unheard-of low prices.

In an era of double-digit interest rates, its customers paid membership fees up front, which slashed capital costs. The store was designed to be cheap to run and it turned its merchandise so rapidly that it could sell goods at or below cost but still make a substantial profit investing the "float."

Club store retailing, as the concept became known, put suppliers in a quandary. Price Club and its imitators often sold goods to its members at prices at or below wholesale. Club shoppers stocked up on household commodities at low unit prices. This incensed competing retailers, whose higher cost structures and merchandising methods precluded competitive response.

As the wholesale club phenomenon spread across the country, shell-shocked conventional retailers delivered ultimatums to brand marketers and manufacturers reps: Don't sell the clubs if you want to keep us as your accounts. Brands were forced to choose between the hot new class of trade and major existing customers who were yielding market share anyway. What's a sales rep to do when he's got a quota to meet?

Just a few years later, about 1981, another crafty merchant named Bernard Marcus presented a revolutionary retail concept before a group of Wall Street investors. His new chain of superstores would sell tools, lumber and other building supplies at the lowest prices possible. Incredulous stock analysts repeatedly asked him whether Home Depot anticipated achieving "better" gross margins as its business grew.

"You must understand," Marcus calmly responded, "For us, a better margin is a lower margin. We want to sell as much volume as possible. We make our money on the turn."

Two decades before the birth of Price Club and Home Depot, another crafty retailer, E.J. Korvette, shook up the status quo in the appliance industry in similar fashion. It too relied at first upon the concept of "membership" to circumvent so-called "fair trade" laws, which had let manufacturers set minimum retail prices for such items as clothes washers and TVs.

Discounting, as this new retail practice came to be called, survived bitter court challenges in the 1960s to revolutionize the marketplace for those goods. This eventually changed the retail margin structure for a host of categories, ranging from recorded music to blue jeans. Discounters favored volume, and turnover, over high markups.

"How do we do it?" went the sales pitch of the day, "Volume!" They stacked 'em high, and watched 'em fly.

As anyone who has ever visited Bentonville, AR knows, today the story of retail innovation is about the shrewd manipulation of price, volume, gross margin and merchandise turnover. In this game, the lowest-cost operator wins, and the manufacturer who supplies the winner is rewarded with market share.

Some would say that Wal-Mart and Price Club embody the theoretical limits in the progression toward low-margin retailing. But there are expenses that remain to be cut. Labor, transportation, real estate and shrink all cut into each chain's profit potential. These costs all relate to a part of the retailing process which may be called fulfillment. Vstore operators are betting that they can be at least partly circumvented, and the resulting savings plowed into home delivery services, lower prices, higher profit margins or all three.

Is Grocery the 'Killer App'?

There is strong precedent for this degree of change in the books and recorded music category, where Amazon.com and CDNow have made significant inroads. Also, the notable successes of the direct-sale computer manufacturers, especially Dell Computer Corporation and Gateway 2000, are a clear demonstration that consumers are willing to make substantial purchases over the Internet, where they see value or benefit.

Amazon.com sold $147 worth of books and other items on its site last year. Dell sold a cool $1 billion worth of computers, although just about 10% was to consumers (the rest are business customers). Major retailers like Sears and Wal-Mart have also made significant commitment to Web-based selling, the latter with some 80,000 SKUs offered at last report.

There are scores of other examples from outside the grocery arena, but none of them have the potential to do what on-line grocery retailers might do. A consumer may purchase 20 books in a year from Amazon.com — worth maybe $500 in sales. She may buy a computer from Dell once every three years — a $2,500 purchase. But the Vgrocer's target household buys upwards of $5,000 per year worth of groceries, and they buy every week, every year for a lifetime.

This spells an enormous opportunity for the on-line grocers, who can use computing power to turn each of their member households into "locked in" customers. Automatic replenishment, once the sole realm of technically advanced suppliers and business customers is about to come within the reach of the household pantry.

If this seems far-fetched, consider the tens of thousands of consumers in the Northeastern U.S. who heat their homes with oil burners. Many of us (I include my own home in this) purchase heating oil on a plan, which is managed by the oil company. It's automatic: they track our usage, deliver before the tank (i.e. inventory) gets too low, and send the bill.

Consider the convenience of having major household staples automatically replenished the same way. In a home delivery concept like Streamline's which incorporates refrigerated storage, even perishables may be reordered this way.

This is the point the major analysts seem to be missing. They neglect to consider the total lifetime value of a customer in handicapping the Vstore categories. They ignore factors like turnover and repeat purchases. They barely consider the database marketing potential which unfolds once households change their habits and do a significant portion of their grocery shopping on-line, or how the marketing feedback that generates will drive on-line sales even further.

And I believe they miss one other important factor in their analyses. It's what the computer software industry calls the "killer app" or killer application, a software product which would give millions of households a powerful reason to use their computers in daily life.

For business in the mid-1980's, the spreadsheet program Lotus 123 was a "killer app" that drove PC's into offices around the world. For consumers — especially women — in the late 1990s, virtual shopping could well be the "killer app." And grocery is certainly the killer category.

What other activity has greater potential to become part of the fabric of weekly life for homemakers? What other category of shopping is more needed, and less enjoyed? Expect grocery to drive the business within two years, not lag behind it.

In terms of total economic impact, Vstore retailing will quickly eclipse club stores, which today capture about $50 billion in total sales. Over the next five years, Vstores will easily capture between 5 to 10% of the $1.4 trillion U.S. marketplace for consumer goods. Some observers (myself included) believe it may account for fully one-third of all consumer goods spending in this country by the year 2010, a number approaching half a trillion dollars.

Supermarket retailers, brand marketers, sales and marketing companies, and all the third parties which bring services to this industry had best take stock and develop a strategic response. Someone's going to sell to these virtual retailers — why not your brand?

The industry must anticipate new rules for packaging, pricing, promotion, logistics and delivery. It must learn to handle the new flows of consumer information and integrate home replenishment into the rest of the entire supply chain. For better or worse, virtual stores will have an impact on the entire consumer goods business.

In the autumn of 1996 the exploits of Peapod and Streamline and their ilk were just beginning to capture the imaginations of mass retailers. The following page-one feature article appeared in Brand Marketing *magazine in November of that year. After researching this piece, I could not let go of the idea that a new publication was needed that could exclusively focus on the next class of retail trade.*

VIRTUALLY READY

Thought club stores were the ultimate in low-margin, fast-turn retailing? Wait Until You Plug Into THE NEXT CHANNEL

CALL IT "THE BOSTON V-PARTY." Mass retailing innovation is brewing around this historic Northeast city, as a cadre of pioneering virtual retailers set up shop to meet consumers on-line.

- Grocery wholesaler Hannaford Bros., Scarborough, Maine, opened a dedicated fulfillment center in Auburndale, Mass. Last month to support a new home-delivery service called "Hannaford Homeruns." Consumers will use the service to order groceries via phone or fax, and the company has indicated ordering by computer may be offered at a later date.

- Streamline opened a 56,000 square-foot "consumer resource center" in Westwood, Mass. in October following two years of testing an on-line home delivery service there. Simultaneously, Streamline also announced an agreement with wholesaler Supervalu, Minneapolis, to supply its operations.

- Groceries To Go, Medford, Mass. opened a 4,000 square-foot warehouse facility in August, where home shoppers can drive up to a pickup window to receive their grocery orders, like a fast-food drive-through. About 30 households are participating in the pilot. They place orders via the Internet, and then either make a delivery appointment or pick it up on their own.

- Peapod, the Evanston, Ill.-based on-line grocery shopping service, inked an agreement last summer with retail grocer Stop & Shop to be its source of supply for a Boston-area expansion of its service. Perhaps the best established of the virtual retailers, Peapod currently boasts more than 21,000 users in four markets across the country.

Call them non-store retailers, consumer direct, or virtual stores — these operators all have two things in common: One, they are replacing the physical front end with an on-line communications vehicle — a V-store. Two, they are eliminating large chunks of traditional operating costs and pouring the savings back into delivery services and web sites, while still preserving higher profits than traditional supermarkets.

"That is, to me, the next channel," says Chris Hoyt, president of Hoyt & Co., Stamford, Conn., a marketing consulting firm. "On-line ordering is definitely going to be a major factor in the business."

The Boston-area start-ups are just the tip of the iceberg when it comes to virtual stores. Other V-store operators and start-ups around the country include: Shoppers Express, Bethesda, Md.; Shopping Alternatives, also in Bethesda; Groceries On-Line, New York; Smart Food, Cambridge, Mass.; and Pink Dot, Anaheim, Calif.

Individually, none of these companies amount to a major threat to the mass-retailing status quo. But collectively, the just may represent the next wave in the continuum of retail innovation.

Throughout the history of mass retailing, new, more efficient retail forms have wrested share from older, less-nimble channels which preceded them.

By engineering their businesses for improved sales velocity and lower selling costs, supermarkets displaced traditional grocers; discount chains grabbed share from department stores; club stores took bites out of both supermarkets and mass merchants.

The membership club store, with its big box construction, no frills, high turns, and 7% to 8% gross margin, seemed until now to be the ultimate in retail efficiency. Surely no retail model could cost less to operate — until the V-store.

"To create an even lower-cost channel, the store needs to be cut out of the equation," says Fred Schneider, executive director of Andersen Consulting's Smart Store, Chicago, which has been studying the V-store premise with a group of manufacturers and retailers its calls the "Consumer Direct Cooperative."

"When we separate information from movement and delivery, we find it is not only the most efficient way, it is really the low-cost way to do business."

Andersen won't reveal the specifics of its work on the CDC, which involved 18 brand marketers and retailers, including V-store startup Streamline. However other sources indicate that the group projected on-line retailing would capture an 8% to 12% share of major market grocery sales over the next seven to 10 years. That fraction, the equivalent of $60 to $85 billion in annual volume, would exceed the current business of club stores and supercenters combined.

With the CDC work completed, Schneider agrees that the term "consumer-direct" does not accurately describe the new business models currently being explored by V-store entrepreneurs.

"All these models imply complete de-coupling of information about the products from the physical products themselves," says Schneider, who explains that the business can really be divided into three components: The consumer interface, or virtual store, is purely an information-based activity.

Home delivery or pickup is the middle piece of the business. Order-picking, logistics, and category management make up the back-end piece.

If all three activities are done effectively, there is an opportunity to bring groceries to the consumer at prices which are competitive with existing channels, says Tim DeMello, founder and chief executive officer of Streamline.

"In the future, there will be a disaggregation between physical product and product information," he says. "When we separate information from movement and delivery, we find it is not only the most efficient way, it is really the low-cost way to do business."

DeMello explains that by setting up its physical operations in a warehouse industrial area, close to main roads, Streamline is cutting out all the retail storefront costs associated with traditional retailing.

"So we do not have the associated [selling, general and administrative] expenses," he says.

Hoyt agrees that successful V-stores will offer a value story that is competitive with existing channels: "Direct-home-delivery will attack the mass consumer, offering a steady stream of staples at the lowest possible price, possibly a price that mass cannot match."

Bypassing the physical retail store offers operational costs savings that can be passed along to consumers, says Alexandra Vo, a principal at Smart Food, a V-store operator that is preparing to open a pilot business in Santa Clara, Calif. "We say to consumers, 'If you order from us you will save time and effort.' Our prices will be competitive and delivery will be free."

Meanwhile, Shopping Alternatives has also compiled a track record in several markets by teaming up with retailers. It too has a business in the Boston area, where it works with Shaw's Supermarkets to offer a service called Shaw's PC Shopper, says Kevin Sheehan, president.

"Until the consumer gets comparable value to what they are getting today, it won't take off," says Sheehan. "This will be the most talked-about retail channel."

Who's Who in V-Stores

Here's a partial list of who's doing what in nonstore retailing:

Groceries On-Line

Where: New York

What: Internet-based home shopping. Graphic-based system demo is completed and will debut in about a month. Has supermarket clients/suppliers lined up in three markets. Company also produces the *Internet Grocery Report*, on-line, an Internet service with about 2,000 retail and manufacturer executives subscribing.

Groceries To Go

Where: Medford, Mass.

What: Internet-based home shopping, integrated with 4,000 square-foot facility for order picking and customer pick-up, similar to a fast-food drive-through. Currently supplied by Star Markets. Pilot operational since August, 1996 and is now handling about 30 customers. Also developing a home-deliver option using own vehicles.

Home Runs

Where: Auburndale, Mass.

Who: Hannaford Bros., Scarborough, Mass.

What: Depot-based virtual store, using phone and fax ordering and dedicated fulfillment center. Company indicated it may eventually offer computer-based ordering as well. Opened in October, 1996.

Peapod

Where: Evanston, Ill. Currently offers services in Chicago; San Francisco and San Jose, Calif.; Columbus, Ohio; and Boston markets in cooperation with local supermarket operators. Plans to add three new markets by December.

Who: Independent with venture capital backing from Tribune Co., Ameritech, Providence Journal Co. and others.

What: Integrated home shopping using direct on-line ordering with proprietary software. Orders are picked at local supermarkets and delivered for a fee.

How Big: More than 21,000 member families. Handled $16 million in gross volume in 1995.

Shoppers Express

Where: Bethesda, Md. Services offered in 17 metropolitan markets.

Who: Independent with venture backing from Rho Management.

What: Business started in 1987 as a phone/fax-based service driven by catalogs. More recently, has developed Shopping Link, an Internet-based ordering service for Vons Pavillion stores in Los Angeles and Kroger stores in Dallas.

Shopping Alternatives

Where: Bethesda, Md. Services offered in seven markets.

What: Home-shopping service offering phone, fax and PC-based ordering. Founded in 1994. Works through retailers: "Shaw's PC Shopper" in Boston, Providence, R.I., Hartford, Conn., and Portland, Maine, as well as with Byerly's in Minneapolis, Cub Food Stores in Atlanta, and Shop 'n Save in Pittsburgh. Orders are shopped and delivered to consumer's home for about $10 per order.

Smart Food

Where: Cambridge, Mass. Setting up services in San Jose, Calif.; Boston; and Seattle.

Who: JKoss Technologies, dba Smart Food.

What: Did some pilot work with Kroger supermarkets, now ended. Preparing to launch integrated home shopping service using "depots" of about 10,000 square feet. Internet-based ordering software.

Streamline

Where: Westwood, Mass.

Who: Start-up with venture capital backing from Reliance Group Holdings and G.E. Capital.

What: Fully-integrated home-shopping system using Internet on-line ordering, customized delivery trucks, and a centralized consumer resource center for order consolidation. Offers, secure, nonattended home delivery, to temperature-controlled locker.

When: First consumer resource center opened in October after about two years of development.

During some 18 years as a practicing business journalist, I had experienced every possible form of turndown from prospective interviewees. Probably the most common brush-off generally began with a question like, "Why would I ever want to talk to you about our business?" In 1997 I wrote down a top ten list and posted it by my telephone. Needless to say, I usually got my story:

TOP TEN REASONS WHY YOU SHOULD TALK TO THE TRADE PRESS

10. Personal ego gratification.

9. To help find yourself another job.

8. To give public credit to the dedicated people who work hard for you and your company.

7. To drive up your stock price or stop it from falling.

6. To amplify or counter things other people are saying about your company.

5. To attract outside talent to come work for your company.

4. To dazzle the boss and get promoted.

3. To practice working effectively with the media — in case one day it really becomes necessary.

2. To ensure that the company's voice is represented in coverage of your industry.

1. Because you may learn something useful from the reporter.

COMPANIES AND BRANDS CITED

ACKNOWLEDGEMENTS

THIS VOLUME would not have come into existence if not for the many friends, colleagues and especially family members who showed their faith in the essential rightness of my concept for *VStoreNews* and in my ability to bring the dream to fruition. Many of these people helped in both tangible and intangible ways and they deserve to share in the satisfaction that I have derived from the experience of building this franchise.

Let me take this opportunity to thank the many talented and influential editors who published my writings, and my many other esteemed colleagues in the business press who have over the years been my mentors, team mates and competitors.

Special thanks are also due to my life-partner Mindy, our sons Joel and Philip, my parents Joan and Arthur Tenser, Steve Kirschner, Stephen Chakwin, Don Ganguly, Rick Dutta, Don Herner, Dale Buss, and Bruce Sloane.

About The Author

JAMES ("JAMIE") TENSER is a career business journalist who was dragged by the Internet retailing phenomenon into consulting and entrepreneurship. His work focuses especially on online business strategy for retail and consumer products companies. He is founder in 1998 and editor of *VStoreNews* and vstorenews.com, which provide retailers and brand marketers with analysis and strategic insight about virtual retailing.

His present obsession grew out of a distinguished 20-year career as a business journalist, analyst and commentator covering consumer goods retailing and marketing for business publications including *Brand Marketing*, *Supermarket News*, *Discount Merchandiser* and *VisionMonday*.

Tenser is frequently quoted in national and international media and trade publications. He regularly contributes columns to magazines such as *Chain Store Age*, *RetailTech*, *Executive Technology*, *Brand Marketing*, and *eRetailing World*. He has made numerous television and radio appearances, and is a frequent speaker at industry trade shows and conferences, including Internet World, iGrocer, Retail Systems 2000, the International E-Commerce Congress (Germany), Grocery Manufacturers of America Internet Marketing Conference, e-Retail '99.

Although he has written thousands of published articles, this is his first book.

Tenser received his undergraduate degree from Cornell University and studied Media Ecology as a post-graduate at New York University.

He may be contacted by email at jtenser@vstorenews.com

www.ingramcontent.com/pod-product-compliance
Lightning Source LLC
Chambersburg PA
CBHW051243050326
40689CB00007B/1046

* 9 7 8 0 7 5 9 6 3 8 0 4 4 *